AF413753

FOR COACH

An Inspiring True Story of Tragedy and Triumph

NANCY BAUER

First Printing, 2022

Bauer, Nancy
For Coach: An Inspiring True Story of Tragedy and Triumph
ISBN: 979-8-9861340-0-0
1. True stories 2. Death and loss 3. High school football 4. Faith
5. Divine Providence

In loving memory of
Craig Crespino
September 23, 1960 - July 21, 2006

CONTENTS

Acknowledgments

For Coach was a collaborative effort of many people whose lives were forever changed that fateful summer of 2006. I want to thank my husband Blaise, first and foremost, for his support and encouragement, but also for the many hours he spent with me once I decided to put pen to paper: re-watching game films, describing the season, recalling the impact that Craig Crespino's life and death had on our community. Blaise and I always knew we had been part of something incredibly profound that fall, and for many years wished for someone to write an account of Craig's legacy and the events following his death so they would never be forgotten. Somehow at some point that someone became me.

Very early in the writing process I realized that Blaise and I held only a fraction of the story. The Crespino family kept the most pertinent memories. Words cannot express my gratitude to Glenna Crespino for being willing to reopen that terribly painful chapter of her life and share with me—and you—her darkest and most private moments. Glenna compiled all information regarding their early years, Craig's accomplishments and pet projects, and his impact on friends and neighbors. She also encouraged me to keep writing when I was ready to hand the project over to a professional author. This book would not have been possible without her contributions and encouragement.

I want to thank Erica and Anthony Crespino for sharing their memories. Their only request of me was that the story be about their father's life—not just his death. I hope that I have successfully captured who Craig Crespino was, the almost unbelievable number of lives he touched, and the amazing legacy he left behind. Craig's parents, Frank and JoAnn

Crespino, were also very gracious in sharing the details of their heartbreaking loss, and for that I am truly grateful.

At the risk of leaving someone out, I also owe thanks to the following people for their contributions: Jace Cobb, Tyler Bennett, Ben Paoni, Tyler Edwards, Trent Crask, Jacob Smith, Mike Cook, Nick Cheney, Joseph Clark, Jeremiah Hudson, Craig Siebert, Dave Wutke, Dr. Adam Paoni, Faith Paoni, John and Clara Black, Dr. James "Chris" Christman, Officer Jeff McDonald, and Dustin Johnson.

Special thanks to Mary Jane Dent for her editing expertise. During her 41 years at Girard High School, Mrs. Dent taught English, was library media specialist, served as journalism advisor, and was a friend and colleague to Craig and Blaise.

Prologue

In the course of a lifetime, only a handful of happenings impact our lives so profoundly that we never forget where we were when we first received word of the news. For anyone living in or around the small town of Girard, Kansas, during the summer of 2006, the tragic and completely unexpected death of Girard High School head football coach Craig Crespino will forever be one of those events.

Coach Crespino's death, just three days before the GHS football camp was to begin, ravaged the tight-knit community. But for the high school football players who were gearing up for a promising season, it left them without their leader, their father-figure, and their most ardent advocate.

Craig Crespino seemed to know everyone in southeast Kansas. He genuinely loved people and had an extraordinary ability to make others feel important and cared about—especially the students at Girard High School. Affectionately known to them simply as "Coach," Craig loved them all like his own. He became a teacher and coach so he could impact the lives of young people, and he most certainly did that.

For Coach is the true story of Craig Crespino: his life, his death, and his legacy. It's the story of Craig's good friend, Blaise Bauer, GHS high school principal at the time, and his mission to help the school, the players, and the community heal. It's an account of lives intertwining in a manner so uncanny one might suspect a higher power had orchestrated their convergence. A tale of the unbelievable—somewhat unexplainable—series of events that followed the devastating loss. And it's the story of the high school football team that set out to honor their fallen coach in the only way they knew how.

By winning.

CHAPTER 1

Welcome to Girard

"When I think of positive ripples made by human beings and the effects they have on people and a community, I think of Coach Crespino. He helped make Girard a very special place and though his life was short, his kindness, care, and influence will echo into eternity in the hearts and minds of people he touched."
– Brad Herlocker, GHS Class of 1994 and GHS head girls' basketball coach, 2006-present

The small town of Girard, Kansas, sits quietly in the southeastern corner of the state. With a population of around 2,800, it's a very rural town, even for Kansas. The community is decidedly agricultural, largely dependent upon its local farming families. Because it's the county seat, Girard boasts a lovely stone-clad courthouse on its quaint town square, around which the community's annual Fall Festival is held.

Residents of Girard know their neighbors. Children ride their bikes down tree-lined streets without worry. Multiple generations farm the family ground. Gossip in town is kept to a minimum, primarily because anyone you might share it with is probably somehow related to the subject of the enticing tale. Life is just a little slower in Girard, and that's the way folks like it. It isn't Mayberry, but it's good. Wholesome. A great place to call home—as noted by the signs that welcome visitors to the community.

The town was once a cultural hub of socialist politics. In the early decades of the twentieth century, the largest-circulating socialist newspaper in U.S. history was published and shipped out of Girard. Notable politicians, authors, and activists from all over the country were regular visitors to the prominent town. Its proud, bustling square featured swanky hotels, fashionable department stores, and multiple opera houses.

But by 2006, the only politics being discussed in the sleepy little town were who was running for mayor, or perhaps city council, when the next elections rolled around. In contrast to once regal businesses, the town square had been reduced to an eclectic mix of mom-and-pop shops. Several of the historic buildings sat empty, patiently pining for someone to usher them into the next chapter of their ever-changing existence.

Girard's tidy lattice of streets had only one traffic light, a flashing four-way stop just a few blocks north of the town square at the intersection of Summit and St. John streets. The two roads were among only a handful in town that did not fizzle into gravel the minute you left the city limits, which apparently warranted a stoplight at their convergence. Girard had no big chain stores and only a handful of locally owned restaurants. The county fair was the biggest event of the year, and even the high school homecoming queen could be seen proudly showing livestock there.

Small towns love their schools, and Girard is no exception. In 2006, not a single team state championship trophy graced the cases of Girard High School, but the community loved and supported their kids regardless. On crisp, fall Friday nights the bleachers overlooking Frank Jameson Football Field were full of loyal Trojan fans. Come spring, nearly everyone in town came out to watch the high school students promenade into the gym on prom night. And there was never a shortage of support for any school fundraiser, whether it was chili night at the high school basketball game or a PTO function at the elementary school. The Girard community revolved around its schools.

Girard High School had around 300 students in 2006. The school sat just blocks from the town square. It was an old building, relatively speaking, and through the years there had been talk of building a new high school on the outskirts of town. Most residents agreed, however, that Girard High School was right where it should be—in the center of town, near the heart of the community.

Girard folks looked forward to National FFA (Future Farmers of America) Week when GHS students were invited to drive their tractors to school. A colorful profusion of farm machines in the school's east parking lot greeted motorists traveling down Summit Street and invariably elicited a smile. Parents loved that the high school's south lot was the postgame hangout for the students, and the fact that the administration was just fine with that. Community members appreciated the district's rather strict hair policy and dress code. Even the students didn't seem to mind them much, considering the natural defiance of teens.

One of Girard High School's most beloved assets was their exuberant head football coach, Craig Crespino. The 45-year-old was an icon in the close-knit community. Having coached the GHS Trojans for 22 years, the gregarious teacher and coach was nothing short of a local celebrity. He and his family seemed to know everyone in southeast Kansas.

The Crespinos relished their life in Girard. Craig and his wife Glenna, also a teacher, had close friends and jobs they were passionate about. The couple would be celebrating 25 years of marriage soon and were hoping to do something special for the occasion. In the summer of 2006, their daughter Erica was preparing for her senior year of college at Wichita State University. Their son Anthony had just graduated from high school and would be attending nearby Pittsburg State University in the fall. Everything was coming together for their family in a way that felt to them like perfection.

As the summer break waned, Craig and Glenna decided to make one last trip to Wichita to visit Erica before school resumed and football season consumed the Crespino household once again. Before they could leave that Friday afternoon, Craig had a few tasks to tend to in preparation for the team's summer football camp, which was to start Monday, and Glenna had plans with friends. The couple would reconvene at the house a little after noon and be on their way.

It was just an ordinary morning for the Craig Crespino

family. Busy, but good. Simple, but gratifying. Modest, but valuable. Authentically wholesome life in a quiet, rural town in the heartland. Girard, Kansas, was small-town living at its best. Life was simple and good there. Things were as they should be.

Perhaps that fact—that things were as they should be in the idyllic town of Girard—is what made the terrible accident that hot July morning all the more devastating for the unsuspecting community.

CHAPTER 2

Life, Love & Family

"Craig was such a good friend in high school. He seemed to know when I was having a bad day, and he would take the time to just say, 'Hey, what's going on?' He was a very good role model for the whole student body."
- Linda Vacca Wosel, St. Mary's Colgan Class of 1979

Craig Joseph Crespino, the firstborn son of Frank and JoAnn (Ferns) Crespino, was born September 23, 1960, a warm fall day in the heart of the Missouri high school football season. It was only fitting that Craig's life began in the midst of something that would forever bring him joy. At the time Craig's father, Frank, was head football coach at El Dorado Springs High School. The young coach's enthusiasm for the game and his natural rapport with his players made him an instant success.

Just months after the birth of their son Craig, Frank and JoAnn took notice when the job of head high school football coach opened at their alma mater, St. Mary's Colgan Catholic Schools in Pittsburg, Kansas. Enticed by the opportunity to return to a parochial environment, Frank eagerly applied. When he was offered the position, the young couple was excited to rejoin their Catholic community in Pittsburg, a growing college town in the southeastern corner of the state.

Frank took on his new role with a passion, and the Crespinos quickly became Colgan royalty. In his 18-year tenure at the helm, Frank's only losing season as head football coach was his first. Coach Frank Crespino and his formidable Colgan Panther football teams put the small Catholic school on the map. In 1974, he took his team all the way to the state championship game and for the first time in school history brought home the state title. He would do the very same thing the following year, a feat which led to his selection as 1975 Kansas Coach of the Year.

The Crespino family enjoyed life in Pittsburg. Craig and his brother, Curt, thrived in the familial atmosphere of St. Mary's Colgan schools. A football fanatic himself, Craig grew up in the bosom of the beloved game and reveled in the limelight of his esteemed father. In the late '70s, Craig was excited to have the opportunity to play high school football under Frank. The two had always shared a close bond and a mutual respect, which made the player-coach relationship work.

"Coaching your own son can be difficult," Frank once told a local reporter. "You have a tendency to be harder on your own kids."

Craig proved to be extremely coachable, however, and had

a strong work ethic as well. By the beginning of his senior year, the coaching staff agreed that he had earned the position of starting quarterback. Frank and Craig looked forward to Craig's senior season with genuine fervor. Having a mutual love for the game of football, they knew the time spent together as father-son, coach-player would be something they would always treasure.

Among the most highly anticipated games that season—and every season for the Colgan Panthers—was the matchup against their neighboring rival, the Frontenac Raiders. The small town of Frontenac, Kansas, sits immediately north of Pittsburg. The two communities share a common boundary for a little over a mile, although Pittsburg is considerably larger in both population and area.

In 1978, Frontenac High School had a new head football coach named Joe Clark. The young coach, himself a former Frontenac Raider, had been part of Frank Crespino's coaching staff during his student teaching experience at St. Mary's Colgan a year earlier. While Joe was an assistant coach under Frank, Craig had been introduced to Joe's younger sister Glenna, and the connection was immediate.

Craig and Glenna began dating the summer before their senior year. The young couple didn't let their schools' rivalry get in the way of their budding romance. They made mutual friends, and spent every weekend attending school activities and enjoying the high school revelry. Date nights often revolved around Craig's other love, football. Craig and Glenna and their friends spent many evenings at the Crespino home watching old football reels on a white sheet hung on the living room wall.

It was a magical time, as senior years should be. But as fall turned to winter and winter to spring, the countdown to graduation began, and the couple looked to the future. Glenna had aspired to be a teacher for as long as she could remember. She was excited to begin that journey at the local university in Pittsburg. Formerly Kansas State College of Pittsburg, the school had recently been granted university status and was now Pittsburg State University. Glenna knew their education program was outstanding.

A baseball scholarship in the Kansas City suburb of Overland Park awaited Craig. The ardent sports fan felt privileged to be able to continue playing ball at the collegiate level. Academically, he had plans to become a doctor, a decision influenced by his uncle, Dr. Fran Ferns, who he greatly admired and respected. Although it meant being two hours apart, Glenna knew that healthcare was something Craig would be good at. He genuinely cared about people and wanted a career where he could help others. She was sure he would make a great doctor.

High school graduation came and went, and summer settled into the Midwest. For Craig this meant baseball season was in full swing. While playing for a local team, he developed a strong bond with his coach and became close with several coaches at Pittsburg State University as well. He was also spending countless hours with his father preparing for next year's football season. Relishing every moment focused on athletics, Craig prayerfully began to rethink his professional goals.

"I'm considering changing my major and going into education and coaching instead," he told Glenna one midsummer day. "I could help a lot of people as a doctor, but you don't develop the same relationships you do as a teacher and coach. We've both had teachers who have made a real impact on us. I want to be able to do that."

During his years as a student athlete, Craig had come to appreciate the influence a good coach could have on his or her players. He had watched his father coach and shape lives. Far beyond X's and O's, coaching provided opportunities to teach life lessons, be a positive role model, and take a group of relative strangers and morph them into a family. Craig recognized that athletics could have a profound impact on the lives of young people and ultimately decided he was meant to be a part of that.

Later that same week, Craig enrolled at Pittsburg State University. He and Glenna were thrilled to be attending the same college and venturing down the same career path. Everything was falling into place, and the couple began talk of getting married after graduation. It was a wonderful and exciting time!

But then came the curve ball. It was January of 1980.

"Glenna?" The voice on the other end of the line trembled. Glenna recognized her mother's voice but could tell something was very wrong.

"What is it, Mom? What's wrong?"

"It's your dad," Shirley Clark began. "They're taking him to KU!"

Glen Clark had been having severe abdominal pains. Local doctors were unable to figure out the source, and his pain was increasing. An ambulance was called, and Glen was rushed to the University of Kansas Medical Center in Kansas City.

Craig quickly drove Glenna to her parents' home in Frontenac. Minutes later Glenna, her mother, and her older brothers Rick and Joe were on their way to Kansas City. The youngest Clark sibling, 10-year-old Mike, stayed behind at a friend's house. The Clark family nervously shared their concerns as they made the two-hour drive north, but they assured themselves that Glen would get the answers and care he needed at KU. The facility had an excellent reputation.

When the family arrived at the large medical center, they made their way to Glen's room, hoping to find him resting comfortably and feeling better. To their dismay, the source of Glen's suffering continued to elude medical staff. Glenna and her family prayed for answers, but none came. Within hours of the family's arrival, Glen Clark was dead at the age of 44. An autopsy later determined he had died of pancreatitis.

Glenna was devastated, knocked from her sturdy foundation by a wave of anguish that thrashed her into jagged rocks of grief and shock. She and Craig mourned the loss together.

"How did this happen? How is it possible that life can take such a drastic turn so suddenly?" Glenna ached. "It's completely unfair."

"Life is short," Craig said sadly. He pulled Glenna to him, his own sense of peace dislodged by the cruel and unanticipated lesson on the brevity of life. "I guess I never really thought about it before, but life is so short. You can't take a single day for granted."

The lesson stuck with the young couple and forever changed their perspective on life, love, and family. The remainder of their freshman year proved difficult. The couple weathered the storm together and leaned heavily on each other as they tried to focus on their studies and their future.

One warm September day, early in their junior year, the two made plans to meet on campus. Glenna's birthday was approaching, and Craig had a gift for her. Glenna opened the box to reveal a beautiful diamond cross necklace. She put it on immediately.

They sat on the front steps of the Newman Center on the PSU campus and talked and talked, right through their afternoon classes. Glenna was still grieving and struggling to cope in the aftermath of her father's death.

"It's so hard to see Mom hurting," Glenna said. "It still hasn't sunk in completely. She's alone now, and I'll never see my dad again. It's awful."

She put her head on Craig's shoulder.

"I think if your dad could tell us anything right now, it would be to enjoy life while you can," Craig began. "Don't wait for the timing to be right. Enjoy every moment."

Craig turned to face Glenna, looking serious and intent.

"I don't want to wait until after graduation to get married. Let's do it now."

Glenna looked at him and smiled quizzically.

"Glenna Clark, will you marry me?"

"Yes!" Glenna responded excitedly, and wedding plans soon began.

The winter of 1982 proved to be one of the coldest in recent history. Brutal arctic blasts pummeled the nation week after week, and long-held record lows were threatened almost daily. In contrast, Sacred Heart Catholic Church in Frontenac, Kansas, was warm and cheery on the afternoon of Saturday, January 9, when Glenna Clark became Mrs. Craig Crespino. Glenna cherished the small, modest ring Craig placed on her finger that day, although he assured her he would buy her a "better one" once they were out of college and had a proper income.

The newlyweds moved into the married dorms on the PSU campus to finish their last few semesters of college. Soon, Craig and Glenna were preparing for their senior year and their student teaching experiences. Craig was assigned to Frontenac High School under Greg Hafner, the current head football coach of the Frontenac Raiders. He was excited to help in the coaching arena as well as gain experience in the classroom.

It was a great year and a positive experience for Craig. He felt right at home at his former rival. When graduation neared in the spring, Craig was offered a position at FHS for the following school year, teaching PE and serving as assistant football coach. The Crespinos were facing their first big decision.

An inner-city school in Wichita had also offered Craig a position, and Glenna had a job offer from a Wichita school as well. The thought of a new community and a new adventure was exciting! However, the loss of Glenna's father had left a powerful impression on the young couple, and remaining close to family was a top priority. After much consideration and prayer, they decided Craig would take the Frontenac position, and Glenna would continue to apply for jobs in southeast Kansas.

Before long, Glenna was offered a third-grade position

at nearby Weir Elementary, around 15 miles southwest of Frontenac. The Crespinos found a small apartment in Pittsburg, which allowed for a short commute for each of them. This first taste of adulthood was exhilarating. Craig and Glenna treasured their life together, as well as the opportunity to finally be in the classroom impacting students. They felt settled and happy. In the spring of 1984, however, an opportunity arose which would alter the trajectory of the Crespinos' lives forever.

CHAPTER 3

Making Girard Home

"It was the first time I had a coach seem genuinely interested in us as individuals. He was personable, and I never felt like he did it just for the stipend."
- Kim Pitts, GHS Class of 1989

"Craig Crespino?" The voice on the other end of the line was strong and confident.

"Yes, sir," Craig answered.

"This is John Kotzman calling from Girard High School."

The head football coach and athletic director was hoping to entice Craig to leave Frontenac for a teaching and coaching position at GHS.

A short 13 miles northwest of Frontenac, Girard had a reputation as a rural, farming community with excellent schools. Craig and John enjoyed a friendly conversation about football, education, and the Girard community. In the end Craig was convinced to apply and was ultimately offered the position. It was an opportunity the Crespinos could not refuse, and soon they were making plans to call Girard, Kansas, home.

Craig and Glenna excitedly purchased the house that the Girard High School Building Trades students were constructing that summer as part of a special project. It was a quaint three-bedroom home on a corner lot on one of Girard's main streets. With a steady supply of traffic, the location was perfect for Craig, who never met a stranger. Homey and inviting, the charming little house beckoned to passersby to stop in for a visit.

The Crespinos quickly made friends in Girard. Coach Kotzman and his wife Beth were among the first, but all of the coaches and their wives were almost instantly like family. Craig was hired to help coach several sports at GHS and was eager and excited for every opportunity to work with young people. He immediately loved Girard—the community, the staff, and, of course, the students. And Girard loved the Crespinos. It was an absolute fit!

Even before the new school year started, Craig began preparing for the Girard Trojan football season. He spent hours poring through the defensive playbook, collaborating with fellow coaches, and studying new schemes and techniques. Craig lived and breathed football, and the game fed his soul. His high energy and enthusiasm for the sport were positively contagious, and he relished time with those who enjoyed the game as much as he did.

Beyond the coaching preparations, Craig spent a great deal of time getting to know the students. His genuine interest in them inspired many students to participate in athletics. One would be hard-pressed to find a former player who didn't have a story about Coach Crespino stopping at his or her house to visit. The conversations were very often not even about sports. They were more likely about whatever was important to that student at that time. Coach Crespino loved and cared about his students, and they knew it.

Craig taught physical education, weight lifting, and social studies classes at Girard High School, and served as a class sponsor and Student Council sponsor. He coached freshman girls' basketball and helped coach track, baseball, and, of course, football. Football was certainly his favorite, but one would never know that he didn't love the other sports with equal fervor. Everything he poured himself into received his absolute best, and he ran at one speed: high energy.

GHS students loved Coach Crespino's outgoing personality and his perpetual smile. He made every student feel important. Boy or girl, athletic or not, scholastically gifted or musically inclined, it didn't matter to Craig. They were all "his kids."

The Crespinos settled into life in Girard with ease, and soon began talk of starting a family. Every young couple has qualifications as to when the time is right to have children, and the Crespinos had decided to wait until they had a backyard. With the purchase of their new home, the timing was right. The two were giddy with excitement when Glenna quickly became pregnant.

"Look at my fingers," Glenna said to Craig midway through the pregnancy. She held up her hand and bared her puffy, swollen fingers. "I can hardly get my wedding ring on."

The swelling continued, making it a struggle for Glenna to wear the ring. Craig came home from football practice one day to find his wife upset.

"I can't find my ring! I've had to take it off so many times because of this swelling, I don't know where I put it." Glenna was heartbroken.

"Well, if it doesn't turn up, we'll just buy you a new one. I promised to buy you a better one someday anyway." Craig hugged her tight. They both suspected the ring was gone for good.

The Crespinos put the crib together in March of 1985 during spring break. It proved to be just in time. On March 27, two weeks before her due date, a baby girl was born to the happy couple. Craig chose the name Erica, and she was her daddy's darling. He called her "Little Miss Am-Erica." Craig and Glenna were over-the-moon in love with their sweet little bundle, and their joy in being new parents was indescribable.

A few short years later, Glenna became pregnant again. By the spring of 1988, Glenna was overdue and feeling huge. On March 23 they hosted an early birthday party for Erica, whose third birthday was less than a week away. Grandparents Frank and JoAnn Crespino attended Erica's party. Frank had since left St. Mary's Colgan High School and was now the principal at Weir Elementary where Glenna was teaching.

"I really don't think you should go to school tomorrow," Craig told Glenna that evening. Frank agreed, and the two convinced the expectant mother to begin her maternity leave immediately. It was a fortuitous decision. Glenna went into labor the following afternoon. At 3 p.m. she drove herself to Girard High School and parked next to the outdoor basketball court where several students were playing ball. The boys watched Glenna get out of the car and immediately knew she was in distress.

"We'll go get Coach!" they yelled. Glenna nodded and wriggled arduously into the passenger seat of the vehicle.

A few hours later, on March 24, 1988, a baby boy was born to the Crespinos. Craig and Glenna named him Anthony. The couple now had a girl and a boy, and their little family felt complete.

Growing up in Girard was simply grand for the Crespino children. Their larger-than-life father was loved by all, and they were treated likewise. Coaches' children in general tend to be "adopted" by the entire community, an acknowledgement of the hectic lifestyle of a coach's family. It's a safe, nurturing, loved existence.

As a toddler, Anthony was in his element on the sidelines with his charismatic father. His daycare was directly across a dead-end street from the high school practice football field. The youngest Crespino would spend fall afternoons pressed against the front screen door, eagerly waiting for the boys to start arriving for practice. Once he spotted them, Anthony would ask to join his father on the practice field, and Glenna would get a phone call from the sitter.

"Hi, Glenna. Someone would like your permission to walk across the street and join his dad at football practice!"

The two women would chat a minute, and then the toddler would be allowed to run over to the practice field. The situation was ideal.

Anthony loved hanging out on the sidelines with the football players and team trainers. One year for his birthday, he informed his parents that he wasn't interested in inviting the other daycare children to his party. He only wanted to invite his favorite high school football players. Although a bit leery of the outcome, Glenna sent party invitations to Anthony's favorite players. She made a cake, and the family put up birthday decorations. Then they waited. Right on time, the football players showed up bearing gifts. Anthony could not contain his joy and excitement. For that matter, neither could his parents.

Glenna continued to commute to Weir Elementary while their children were very young. Once Erica started preschool, however, she wanted to be in Girard with the rest of her family. In 1989, she applied for a first-grade position at Girard's R.V. Haderlein Elementary and was offered the job. Now just blocks from their charming little home on the corner, Glenna could almost walk to work—a welcome change from her years of commuting. Being in the same building as Erica, with little Anthony just a few blocks away at daycare, brought the working mother a great deal of peace as well.

With Glenna in Girard, Craig would leave the high school on his lunch break to pick up a Sonic hamburger with no bun, an iced tea (with many packets of Sweet'N Low), and a Dr. Pepper for Glenna. He would go to her classroom for a couple of minutes each day to deliver her drink and snatch a kiss. If Glenna happened to be out of her classroom during his visit, Craig would leave her drink on her desk, along with a note that said, "I love ya."

Having the entire family in the same school district was a dream come true for the close-knit Crespinos. They had made good friends in Girard, and their parents and extended family were nearby as well. It was everything they had hoped for, and they felt extremely blessed.

CHAPTER 4

The Coaching Family

"Mrs. Crespino was my second-grade teacher, and Coach would bring her a Sonic drink almost every day and occasionally some flowers or some form of candy surprise. I always knew that was the kind of love I wanted to have!"
- Ashlyn Sandberg, GHS Class of 2012

In addition to their new elementary teacher, Girard schools welcomed a new high school teacher in the fall of 1989 as well. Blaise Bauer had spent the previous spring semester doing his student teaching under John Kotzman, Craig Crespino, and science instructor Dick Fogliasso, and had recently been hired to teach biology at Girard High School. He had just graduated from Pittsburg State University where he was a standout on the football team.

Blaise grew up in Monett, Missouri. He attended Catholic grade school but later transferred to Monett's public high school. The move was necessary to participate in sports, which was a priority for him. Supported by a single teacher's salary, the eight children of Leonard and Barbara Bauer didn't take anything for granted. Money was tight, and throughout their high school years they worked hard to earn scholarships to pay their way through college.

A lifelong Arkansas Razorbacks fan, the confident and athletic high school graduate enrolled at the University of Arkansas in hopes of earning a spot on the football team. Blaise redshirted his freshman year, which gave him an extra year of eligibility. It also gave him an additional year to work hard and hone his skills. His talent and work ethic did not go unnoticed, and Blaise felt sure that he would see the field at some point.

But fate, or perhaps the Lord, had other plans. In the summer of 1985, after completing his freshman year at the University of Arkansas, Blaise received a phone call from Dennis Franchione, who happened to be Glenna Crespino's uncle. Coach Franchione had just been hired as the new head football coach at Pittsburg State University and was on a mission to recruit some fresh talent.

"Arkansas wants you, but we need you," Franchione told Blaise. "I can offer you some scholarship money."

Blaise was making definite gains at the University of Arkansas but still had not been offered an athletic scholarship. He was receiving limited financial assistance, but it did not cover the cost of tuition at the larger school. The thought of giving up his dream of playing for the Razorbacks was disheartening, but the idea of seeing immediate playing time did appeal to him. He was not necessarily happy about the decision, but in August of 1985 he transferred to Pittsburg State University—the only college in the nation with a gorilla for a mascot.

Humble and grounded, Blaise was liked and respected by his teammates and coaches. They appreciated his strong work ethic and enjoyed his easy, country mindset and thick, southern drawl. An avid raccoon hunter, Blaise endured his share of good-natured ribbing from his teammates about his unusual hobby. He made fast friends, however, and soon felt right at home in southeast Kansas.

Blaise started all four years under Coach Franchione. An outstanding tight end, he set several school records and was a two-time All-Conference and All-American player. During his four years at PSU, the MIAA football powerhouse program compiled an almost unbelievable 45-4 record. The move to PSU had proved to be a good one for the young man.

In May of 1989, Blaise graduated from Pittsburg State, married his college sweetheart, Nancy Backes, and accepted a job at Girard High School. The newlyweds rented a house on the northwest corner of Girard and settled in, excited to begin their lives together. Along with the Kotzmans, the Crespinos were among the first to welcome the Bauers to the Girard community.

Craig and Blaise were kindred spirits. Their competitiveness and love for the game of football transcended reason, and the two could spend hours discussing the various aspects of the game. Blaise was a valuable addition to the Trojan coaching staff and promptly became part of the coaching family.

Craig served as defensive coordinator under head coach John Kotzman, and Blaise took on the role of offensive line coach. The two were in their element on the football field. For both the game was so much more than a game. It was a brilliantly designed chess match, providing coaches the opportunity to take the pieces they were given and orchestrate moves that would exasperate their opponents. It was strategy and adjustments, capitalizing on strengths and minimizing weaknesses.

More importantly, the game instilled self-discipline and developed work ethic. It was a means of establishing lifelong relationships with players and coaches. It was winning with grace and losing with dignity, working as a team, and having your brother's back.

It was life.

In the spring of 1992, Craig came home with news.

"It's official. John's resigning his coaching duties."

He was referring to GHS head football coach John Kotzman. The news was bittersweet. Craig had become like a son to John, and the two had thoroughly enjoyed coaching together for the past eight years. However, John had groomed his good friend for the head coaching job and had recommended him to be his successor.

"You've always wanted to be a head coach," Glenna said, giving him a hug. "It's a great opportunity!"

The school board approved the hire, and Craig began preparing to take the reins as head football coach of the Girard Trojans. The Crespinos didn't think their life in Girard could get any better, but they smiled at their new set of circumstances and realized it just had.

One of Craig's first calls after accepting the position was

to his friend and fellow coach, Blaise Bauer. The two met to discuss the next football season. Craig had served as defensive coordinator for the past eight years, while Blaise had taken over the duties of offensive coordinator during Coach Kotzman's last couple of seasons. It was an opportunity for the young coach to learn the ropes and had been a perfect fit for Blaise, who had always played on the offensive side of the ball.

"You're not wanting to switch responsibilities, are you?" Blaise asked Craig with a bit of a grin. It wasn't common for a head football coach to be the defensive coordinator. Most head coaches want to be in control of the offense. Changing roles would require both men to learn an entirely new aspect of the game and the team. It was not an easy decision for Craig, but he ultimately determined it made more sense to leave things as they were. He would continue to coach the defense, and Blaise would continue to coach the offense. Although an unusual arrangement, it worked for the two friends.

Along with the other coaches, the duo proved a formidable force. Over the 1992 and 1993 seasons, the Trojans amassed an impressive 18-3 record, claiming the league title two years in a row. During Craig's first year as head coach, he took his team all the way to the state semifinals, coming up one game short of playing for a state championship. It was the farthest any Girard football team had ever advanced into the playoffs, and the community was on fire with enthusiasm for their beloved Trojans!

For GHS students, game night excitement began well before Friday night. On Thursdays, after the sun gave way and darkness settled in, a group of high school students would "toilet paper" the Crespino house. Craig loved the tradition!

He would always step outside to see them and share a laugh. Invariably, one of the students would bring him a Chick-O-Stick or a Tootsie Roll, knowing how Craig loved candy. It was a ritual enjoyed by both the students and their coach, who was always sure to clean up the paper before leaving for school the next day so that it didn't end up in the neighbors' yards.

After the Friday morning yard cleanup, the Crespinos would have breakfast with their good friends John and Clara Black and daughter Kacie at Eastside Cafe on the town square. Craig and John were good friends and spent a great deal of time together. John would ride with Craig to pick up game films and sometimes scout other teams for Craig. The two refereed basketball games in the off-season to stay in shape, make a few extra bucks, and just be together.

Postgame gatherings hosted by various coaches, friends, and community members became a cherished tradition as well. They would eat and talk about the game, relishing the energy and enthusiasm the entire town felt for Trojan football. Once Craig became the head coach, the gatherings were always held at the Crespino home. He wanted to be able to tuck his children into bed and still have that time to relive the game with friends.

Craig thoroughly loved this time with kindred spirits. His enthusiasm on the sidelines did not fade when the game ended. Gathered friends would listen with utter rapture as Craig relived the game, the re-creation sometimes more animated and exciting than the game itself. Together they celebrated the victories and supported one another after more disappointing outcomes.

The Crespinos enjoyed their routine and the wonderful

friends they had made in Girard. They would host birthday parties and baby showers for one another. Craig and Glenna were asked to be godparents for a few of the newborns, and their children grew up together. The circle of friends became incredibly dear, and their time together was never taken for granted. They treasured each other far beyond the game of football, and their relationships were the kind that provide a deep inner joy and give the soul peace. Their bonds of friendship were lifelong and life-altering.

CHAPTER 5

Opportunity Knocks

"Coach Crespino made me want more out of life, and made me believe I deserved it."
- Mike Cook, GHS Class of 2007

Although the success of the '92 and '93 seasons was intoxicating, Blaise Bauer was restless. He aspired to be a head football coach, and that was not going to happen in Girard. Coach Craig Crespino was a fixture in the community. He was popular, young, and successful and had no plans to leave anytime soon. That meant the Bauers would have to look elsewhere if Blaise were to have the opportunities he sought.

"The head football job in Galena just opened for next school year," Blaise reported at the supper table one early spring evening in 1994.

His wife Nancy looked up from feeding their youngest, one-year-old Michaela.

"Is there a classroom position available?" she asked.

Blaise shook his head. "Assistant principal."

Nancy's eyes widened. Blaise had recently completed his master's degree in school administration.

"Have you talked to anyone?"

"I did. Called down there today and visited with the superintendent. I like him a lot, and I think I'd really like working with him."

Nancy thought about the opportunity. She understood that Blaise needed to pursue his dream of being a head football coach. She also knew that he eventually wanted to get into administration and that this opportunity would allow him to do both. Still, after five years, Girard felt like home to her. The Bauers' small three-bedroom rental overlooked a rambling pasture and a tranquil fishing pond. They brought their first two children, Gannon and Michaela, home to this house and were now pregnant with their third. A large, shaded yard offered plenty of room for the children to play, and the long, gravel drive gave a sense of safety from passing cars. Nancy enjoyed spending her days with the children in the idyllic setting.

"They'd like for you to come down and visit with them, too," Blaise continued slyly, sensing his wife's reluctance. He peeked over for her reaction. The invitation seemed to win Nancy over, and she smiled at the thought. The following week the Bauers met with the Galena administration, and by the end of the day, Blaise was offered the job of assistant high school principal and head football coach.

"Well, I guess I knew it was going to happen sooner or

later!" Craig smiled and shook Blaise's hand. "I hate to lose you, buddy! But you'll do great things down there. You gotta go for it."

Blaise smiled. He knew Craig was genuinely sad to see him leave Girard High School and their coaching family. The feeling was mutual. Blaise's five years in Girard had been extremely enjoyable. He would miss the small, quiet town and the good, hardworking people who called it home.

"Who knows," Craig continued with a telling grin. "Maybe we'll get you back here one day!"

Moving to Galena, Kansas, from their rural Girard home was an adjustment for the Bauers. About 40 miles south of Girard, Galena hugs the Missouri and Oklahoma borders in the extreme southeastern corner of Kansas. The complete opposite of the peaceful farm community of Girard, Galena in the early '90s was gritty and weathered. Named for the lead ore once mined there, Galena's mining days ended in the 1970s when high lead levels in the soil and water became a health concern for its residents. The town was put on the government's Superfund cleanup list, and its population dwindled to a tenth of its former glory.

When the Bauers arrived in the summer of 1994, Galena was the poorest school district in Kansas, as determined by the Kansas State Department of Education. A number of long-time residents were working hard to revitalize their beloved community, but as in many small towns, generational poverty was taking a toll. Galena's downtown had fallen into disrepair, and a pervasive sense of hopelessness seemed to hang over the tired town. Pride in their community had been choked out of many Galena residents by a struggling economy and an unfortunate drug presence.

Galena's superintendent, Dr. James "Chris" Christman, a Galena native himself, was determined to turn things around. Now in his sixth year as superintendent, Dr. Christman had lofty goals for his hometown. School facilities were being updated and improved, and he had recruited some outstanding new staff. His philosophy was that Galena schools would not accept excuses. They would not lower their expectations to accommodate the less fortunate but would instead insist on hard work and every student's personal best. It was his way of getting the students—and in fact, the entire community—to believe in themselves and set higher goals for their future. Blaise was extremely impressed with his optimism and conviction.

"These kids need good role models and deserve nothing less than the best staff we can recruit," Dr. Christman stated resolutely. He knew that for many Galena students, school was the most positive aspect of their lives. Blaise was sold. Having a genuine heart for kids as well, he had gone into education to impact the lives of young people, and he recognized this as a tremendous opportunity to do just that.

As a whole, Galena's student body was unlike Girard's, a fact that abruptly presented itself to Blaise as he got acquainted. These young people were decidedly more streetwise, and their environment more urban and hard. Many had seen the ugly effects of drugs and alcohol in their homes, and some were engaging in the behavior themselves. Finding a way to make those students care about grades or football was a challenge Blaise had never had to face before.

The Galena Bulldog football team had not had a winning season in over four years. They had lost 28 of their last 36 games and had low expectations for this year's season as well. Losing had become the norm. The players and community had become used to it. Blaise would have to change the team's mindset first and foremost in order to turn things around.

Unfazed by the enormous challenge, the Bulldogs' new head football coach felt confident in his ability to improve the program and give Galena a reason to be proud again. His prowess on the football field and subsequent coaching success had earned him the opportunity to be a head coach for the first time, and he was eager to prove himself and build a winning program in his new community.

Blaise immediately began visiting with the players, meeting their families, and building relationships with them. He established a rapport with the tough, ragtag group of boys, and they respected him tremendously. He didn't talk down to them, but lifted them up. He introduced them to his family. He got to know their parents and their stories. He had high expectations for the boys, but their parents understood that he had the boys' best interests at heart. They trusted him and believed in him. They knew he cared about their kids and wanted them to succeed, both on and off the football field.

The boys came to believe in their new head coach as well. They could see that Coach Bauer wanted to win and that he cared about bringing pride back to their team, their school, and their community. More importantly, they could see that he genuinely cared about them. His investment in them and his commitment to their success convinced them to believe in themselves. And that, with a little bit of raw talent and a handful of creative plays, is sometimes all it takes.

The Galena Bulldogs finished the 1994 season 6-3 under head coach Blaise Bauer. The impressive turnaround led to his selection as Coach of the Year for the CNC (Crawford Neosho Cherokee counties) League. The Bulldogs' six victories included a narrow one-point win over the Girard Trojans. After the game Craig and Blaise made their way to the center of the field.

"Good game, Coach," a smiling Craig Crespino shook Blaise's hand and gave him a hearty hug as well. The friends visited for a long while under the Friday night lights. Blaise eagerly embraced the opportunity to mingle with his former colleagues, players, and patrons. The Bauer family lingered on the field until the lights went out that chilly September evening, enjoying time with the Trojan faithful. Girard would always hold a special place in their hearts.

The Bulldogs donned sharp new uniforms the next year, thanks to Coach Bauer, and the stands were now full in anticipation of another winning season. The team had given the community something to look forward to and something to be proud of. The enthusiasm for the Galena Bulldog football team proved to be an important stepping stone in the town's road to revitalization. Good things were starting to happen throughout the town, and maybe, just maybe, those scrappy boys and their tenacious coach with the engaging drawl had something to do with that.

Blaise served as head coach of the Galena Bulldogs for another four years, compiling a 32-15 record. In 1997, he took the team all the way to the state quarterfinals, a feat which earned him a second CNC Coach of the Year honor. The Galena Bulldogs were now a team to be reckoned with, and pride in the community was growing.

The Bauer family grew during these years as well. Two more daughters, Hayden and Audrey, were born in Galena, bringing their brood to four children ages four and under. These were glorious times for the busy family, but lean ones, too. Blaise and Nancy had made the decision that while their children were little, Nancy would stay at home to raise them. Their cheerful, noisy home was full of love, but this arrangement did make for some tough times.

A propane bill arrived one late winter day that simply could not be paid. Nancy made a difficult phone call to the propane company.

"I need to set up a payment plan for our current balance. Also," she paused, "please take us off the route for the rest of this season."

The Bauers turned the heat down for the remainder of the winter and bundled up. It was not ideal, but they made it work. One night after the children were tucked in their beds, Blaise and Nancy huddled on the couch.

"Maybe it's time I get out of coaching and become a full-time administrator," Blaise offered, knowing a principal's position would bring in more money. "Being a principal is also a goal of mine. I wasn't planning to do it this soon, but maybe it's time."

Nancy looked at him sadly.

She knew how much he would miss the players and the game. Football was in Blaise's blood. He loved coaching the sport, and he was good at it. But more than that, he could reach kids through coaching. He was a good role model for the young men he coached, some of whom desperately needed one.

"Can you be happy not coaching?" she asked.

"I think so." Blaise shrugged, trying to remain positive.

They sat quietly for a moment.

"I'll never tell you that you have to get out of coaching. I can't do that," his somber wife said. "You have to know."

Blaise smiled and held her. "It'll be all right. We'll pray about it."

Eventually, after four years as an assistant principal, Blaise decided to pursue a principal's position. He began as principal of the alternative high school in Galena, which allowed him to continue as head coach of the Bulldogs. However, with four small children at home, Blaise's hectic schedule took a toll, and he realized something had to give. The following year he gave up his head coaching duties at the high school but agreed to coach the eighth-grade football team.

In 2000, Blaise left Galena for a principal's position at neighboring Baxter Springs High School. It would be his first year without coaching duties. He would miss the game of football and the camaraderie among the coaches, but he would miss the players most of all. He wondered if he could have the same relationships with the students as a principal. The move was made for the sake of his family. It was not an easy decision, but he was at peace with it.

Blaise's six years at Galena were some of the most rewarding of his career. He was successful in a place where many told him that was an impossible goal. He had proven himself to be an outstanding coach and administrator, touched the lives of countless young people, and made lifelong friends. Galena was good to the Bauers.

Blaise and Craig stayed in touch through the years, and Craig perpetually reminded Blaise and Nancy that he would one day bring the Bauer family back to Girard. In the spring of 2001, the Girard High School principal announced that he had accepted a job in another district. The position would be open for the upcoming school year. Within hours of the vacancy posting, the Bauers' phone rang.

"We're gonna bring you back home, buddy!" Craig told Blaise excitedly.

CHAPTER 6

Coming Home

"He loved us and trusted us with his children, made us see how a wife and children should be treated, provided laughter and kept secrets when we asked. I have so many fond memories of growing up at the Crespino house."
- Keri (Kotzman) Mick, Crespino family friend; GHS Class of 1990

Not long after Blaise became assistant principal and head football coach at Galena High School, the Bauers had purchased an 1880's farmhouse north of Galena. The family had started in a small house in town but quickly realized they were better suited for the country. The multitude of coonhounds Blaise perpetually owned did not make for good neighbors. The family's "new" residence sat on twelve quiet acres and—being eight miles from Galena—was as far out in the country as Nancy had ever lived. The dwelling was in dire need of repairs, and the Bauers did what they could on a tight budget to make the house a home.

The children attended Spencer Elementary, a small, rural school that sat in a field just a mile or so from their house, as the crow flies. The location was curiously remote but could not have been more perfect for the Bauer family. With fewer than 100 children in the school, Gannon, Michaela, Hayden and Audrey Bauer made up almost five percent of the school's population. Nancy was a regular in the building, an opportunity that being a stay-at-home mom afforded her. She knew every student and staff member by name and considered them her extended family. It was ideal.

Still, the sleepy town of Girard seemed to beckon, like an old friend. The Bauers loved their quiet life in the country, but they lacked a sense of community. Blaise was now the principal in nearby Baxter Springs, Kansas; the children's rural school was in the Columbus, Kansas, district; and the family attended church in nearby Pittsburg or sometimes in Joplin, Missouri. They weren't truly part of any one community and missed that sense of belonging.

When Blaise learned from Craig that the Girard High School principal's position would be open for the 2001-2002 school year, he was excited to apply. Returning to Girard was a carrot the Bauers could not resist. Blaise eagerly went after the open principal's position, and soon the family was making plans to move back to Girard. They purchased a few acres northwest of town and began plans to build a home. Blaise made the one-hour commute from their rural farmhouse while the new house was under construction, and Nancy and the children enjoyed one more year with their Spencer

Elementary family. By the fall of 2002, the Bauers' new home was ready for its anxious residents.

The children started school at Girard's R.V. Haderlein Elementary that August. The family filled the front pew every Sunday morning at St. Michael's Catholic Church in Girard, and Nancy relished being able to volunteer for various roles in the parish. Community, finally. It felt good to be home again. And, of course, the Crespinos were among the first to welcome them back.

Craig was now starting his eleventh year as head football coach. In the eight years the Bauer family had been away, Craig had compiled a 46-21 record, claiming the CNC League Championship twice and earning Co-League Champion status twice. After an 11-1 season in 1999, which included a trip to the state quarterfinals, Craig was named CNC Coach of the Year.

He was also invited to be an assistant coach in the 2000 Kansas Shrine Bowl, a high school summer all-star game which raises money for Shriners Hospitals for Children. The invitation was a tremendous honor for a coach who worked tirelessly every year writing letters of accomplishments for his players, with the hope that they might be selected to participate in the prestigious event. At the conclusion of the 2000 Shrine Bowl game, it was announced that Craig had been selected to return the following year as well, this time as a *head* coach. He was thrilled and humbled to hear his name. The announcement meant a great deal to the entire Crespino family, whose lives revolved around the beloved sport.

Craig's deep-rooted love of the game, his ability to befriend virtually anyone, and his larger-than-life personality made him a tremendous ambassador for high school football in Kansas. He founded the Southeast Kansas Regional Coaches Association, an organization which not only provided professional growth opportunities for area football coaches but also developed positive relationships and a true camaraderie among the coaches. Prior to the group's off-season meetings, these critical elements had been somewhat lacking in the area.

On Saturdays during football season, many of the high school coaches and their families would attend Pittsburg State University football games. The coaches had a designated corner in the stadium, and Craig thoroughly enjoyed the group. The kindred spirits encouraged and supported each other beyond those Saturday afternoons in PSU's Carnie Smith Stadium. When their own seasons came to an end, they would often attend the playoff games of whichever teams were still vying for a state championship and cheer on their friends' programs.

In addition to working to enhance local football, Craig also served as the president of the Kansas Football Coaches Association, an organization that played an important role in shaping high school football across the state. He pushed for a playoff system that would give more teams the opportunity to advance into the playoffs and enable more student athletes to experience the thrill of postseason play. It was what he believed was best for kids. That was always the primary focus for Craig. Ultimately, Kansas did alter their high school football playoff system, allowing two teams from each district—instead of just one—to vie for a state championship.

Craig Crespino was an ardent ambassador for football, for his friends, and for kids. More important to him than any victories or accolades, Craig strove to impact the lives of his students. Many would recount stories of Coach coming to their house when they had experienced difficulties, whether at home or in school. He regularly took students home after practice if they didn't have the means. He made every student feel important. They knew they had a friend and advocate in Coach Crespino. His office door was always open, as was his home. He encouraged them to pursue their dreams, supported them through hardship and disappointment, and offered advice to help them be successful in life. He was like a father to many of his students, and they genuinely loved him.

Craig also found a way to reach Girard's elementary school students. He created the Future Trojan Club and every Friday sent a delegation of his Trojan football players to R.V. Haderlein Elementary to visit various classrooms. The younger students looked up to the boys in awe, and Craig knew their words had the power to make a difference. It was a way of creating community pride and team spirit, but it was also his way of encouraging the Future Trojans to work hard and make good decisions.

Coach Craig Crespino recognized that the game of football had the ability to change lives, and he was determined to impact as many young people as possible through the sport. Coaching football was so much more than a job for him, it was a vocation. Far beyond the game of football, Coach Crespino was a true asset to the Girard community—and, in fact, to all of southeast Kansas.

When the Bauers returned to Girard in the fall of 2002, the Crespino family was gearing up for an especially exciting football season. Their daughter Erica was starting her senior year and was on the high school cheerleading squad. Their son Anthony was now a freshman in high school and was excited to finally play football under his iconic father. Glenna never missed a game that season, freshman or varsity, and Erica was always the first to run out onto the field to hug her dad after every contest. With both Craig and Anthony on the field, Erica cheering them on, and Glenna in the stands, the Crespino family savored every moment of the 2002 football season.

That school year was a joyful blur of family activities while both Crespino children were at GHS. Soon, however, Erica was making plans for life after high school. She had enrolled at Wichita State University and was preparing to move from Girard to the "big city." Craig could barely stand the thought of her being two and a half hours away, but he understood that she had to spread her wings and fly. He would miss her terribly but was also extremely proud of her and wanted her to experience the thrill of independence and the excitement of college life.

As Anthony's sophomore year approached, he came to his father with a difficult decision.

"Hey, Dad," Anthony began. "You got a minute?"

"Of course! What's up?" Craig could tell his son's heart was heavy.

"You know I love football as much as you do, and playing for you is something I've always looked forward to, but I'm just not built for it."

The young man was incredibly disappointed to let go of his dream of playing football, especially for his father. For as long as he could remember, football had been a part of his life. His most cherished memories included the beloved game, whether at Girard High School or Pittsburg State, on road trips to watch Coach Franchione's teams play, or during family trips to the Shrine Bowl. Often it would just be Craig and Anthony, spending quality father-son time together. The two would frequently be invited to stand on the sidelines. Football was part of the special bond they had, and Anthony absolutely loved the game as much as his father. With his tall, lanky frame, however, the high school sophomore knew he was not suited for it and had decided to give cross country a try instead. He wanted to participate in a sport where he could contribute and had conceded that it was time to try something new.

Craig understood completely and respected Anthony's decision, knowing it was not an easy one for his son. Football commitments did not allow Craig to attend many of Anthony's cross country meets, but he was supportive regardless. Anthony excelled at both cross country and track his sophomore year. As an assistant track coach during spring semesters, Craig was thrilled to work with his son in a sport that brought him success.

Craig had to acknowledge that he was feeling a bit restless, however. Erica's absence had affected his focus, and he wondered how much more he would feel the disconnect once Anthony graduated and moved on from GHS. A head football coaching position in a Wichita suburb came available that spring, and Craig was intrigued by the idea of being closer to "his girl." He applied and was offered the job.

The Crespinos did not take the decision lightly. Moving

away from southeast Kansas meant moving away from family. Craig's parents would no longer be able to attend all of his games, and Anthony would have to finish his junior and senior years in a new school. The family weighed the pros and cons, and in the end decided the move was not meant to be.

The following spring, in 2005, another job opportunity presented itself. This time a large Catholic school in the Wichita area was looking for a head coach. Once again, Craig interviewed for the job and was offered the position. He loved and lived his Catholic faith. He had fond memories of attending Catholic schools and watching his father teach and coach at St. Mary's Colgan for so many years. Returning to a parochial environment was something he'd always hoped might be a possibility, and again it was a chance to be closer to Erica, who was still at Wichita State. Craig was extremely interested.

This would be Anthony's senior year, however. Craig thought back to his own senior year and the fun he and Glenna had experienced with friends. Unlike his gregarious father, Anthony was quieter and more reserved. Craig hated the thought of moving him to a school where he would know no one. The Crespinos were terribly conflicted and spent several sleepless nights unsure of what to do.

"Hey, Blaise," Craig began. "Got time to visit?"

Craig reached out to his principal to let him know that he had been offered a job, but mostly he wanted to visit with his friend about the prospect of making such a drastic life change.

Craig and Blaise sat in the Crespinos' living room and discussed the options. Perhaps Glenna and Anthony could remain in Girard for a year so Anthony could graduate with his friends, and the two could move to Wichita after gradu-ation. This certainly was not an ideal arrangement, however, for a family who loved spending time together, and Craig hated the thought of missing most of Anthony's senior year. The decision was proving to be exceedingly difficult.

Glenna could hear the pensive conversation from the kitchen and felt the weight of the verdict on her heart. After more than an hour of discussion, she heard the men praying together. The emotional burden lightened, and she felt at peace. Her faith told her that whatever decision their family made, it would be the right one. The following day Craig declined the job offer. He wanted Anthony to graduate as a Girard Trojan and also wanted to remain close to his parents, who had always been there for him and his family.

Craig and Glenna slept peacefully that night, confident that they were right where they were supposed to be.

CHAPTER 7

The Call

"My first year of coaching, I was introduced to Craig and he treated me like a colleague he had known for years. When I moved to Girard, he made me feel like I belonged, which was big for me because the only other person I knew in town at that time was my wife. He really helped me fit in. I'll always be grateful for the kindness he showed me."

- Brent Myers, former Fort Scott High School track coach

Anthony Crespino was more than a little relieved to be staying in Girard. He looked forward to cross country and track, senior band trips, and good times with friends. In his heart he couldn't imagine his dad coaching any team but the Trojans.

Anthony's senior year was everything he had anticipated,

and before long he and the rest of the GHS Class of 2006 were preparing for graduation. He had a summer job lined up at a local car dealership and would be attending his parents' alma mater, Pittsburg State University, in the fall. Anthony had been awarded a music scholarship and was excited for the opportunity to participate in band at the collegiate level.

Erica Crespino was wrapping up her junior year at Wichita State that spring of 2006. She was working toward a degree in audiology and had her first clinical assignment in Wichita that summer. The internship meant Erica would not be spending the break in Girard as she had in previous years.

Craig and Glenna were incredibly proud of Erica and Anthony, but time together as a family was dwindling as they became adults. Still, the Crespinos were grateful for their decision to stay in Girard. It was home, and they loved that fact. Their lives were full, their kids were happy, and their future was bright. They were at peace.

For the Bauer family, however, an unanticipated complication presented itself early in 2006.

"How does this always happen?" Blaise mumbled to himself, hanging up the phone slowly and deliberately. "Somehow she's always gone when I've got a job decision to make," referring to his wife Nancy, who was out of town with cousins.

Blaise looked out the kitchen window at the large field behind their country home. The brown grass sparkled with a February frost that cold Kansas afternoon. He let out a weighty sigh as he reflected on the phone conversation. The call was unexpected. Out of the blue. An area Catholic school was preparing to make some personnel changes for the upcoming school year, and they were looking for an administrator. They were hoping Blaise would be interested, and he was.

The Bauer family was very happy in Girard and Blaise was not actively looking to make a job change. There was only one set of circumstances that could possibly lure them away—a Catholic school setting.

Blaise grew up in a large, devout Catholic family, and their faith was the center of their upbringing. He and his wife Nancy first spotted each other at Sunday evening Masses at the PSU Newman Center while in college. Now married seventeen years, the Bauers and their four children never missed a Sunday Mass. It was the biggest part of their lives, and they had always anticipated that they would someday be part of a Catholic school community.

When Nancy returned home, the two weighed the decision.

"It's certainly something we've envisioned for our family," Nancy said. She was excited for the opportunity but reluctant to leave Girard. "I hate the thought of moving the kids again, but they'll make new friends and fit in fine."

"We could live here until the house sold," Blaise followed, thinking through the logistical aspects of the move. "The commute is doable."

"What about salary?" Nancy asked. A hint of concern crept into her voice. With four children and one income, salary always had to be a consideration. Blaise felt confident it would not be an issue, however.

"I love how eager they are for you to apply," Nancy smiled.

"But it has to be your decision." She could sense that Blaise was conflicted.

Being sought out felt good. Blaise knew he would enjoy the job and be a good fit. *This is what we've always planned to do,* he kept telling himself. *Where we saw ourselves some-day. So . . . why doesn't it feel right?* He didn't understand the hesitation. It simply did not make sense.

The couple prayed long and hard about it, seeking assurance that the opportunity at the Catholic school was the right move for their family. Instead, Blaise only became more convinced that it was not. Not now, anyway. The intense directive was unlike anything Blaise had ever experienced before. Although he didn't fully understand it, he felt absolutely compelled—perhaps even *divinely called*—to remain in Girard.

Eventually, Blaise picked up the phone and called the parish representative.

"I appreciate your interest in me," Blaise began. "I'm very flattered. My wife and I are both intrigued by the opportunity, but . . . " Blaise looked for the right words as he fumbled to explain. "It's just not what I'm supposed to do right now."

A twinge of regret and uncertainty passed through Blaise as he waited for the man's response, feeling as though he had let him down. To his surprise, a warm sense of acceptance and understanding came from the other end of the line.

"My wife always says, 'Bloom where you are planted,'" the man began kindly. "God just has other plans for you right now."

Blaise smiled and thanked him again for the consideration. It was difficult to let go of the opportunity completely, and he honestly didn't fully understand why he was. But he trusted that, for whatever reason, he was supposed to stay in Girard.

The Bauer family moved forward and tucked the decision away like last season's clothes. They had made the right choice. Girard was home, and—like the spring flowers that would soon be popping up in southeast Kansas—they would bloom where God had planted them.

CHAPTER 8

Summer Bliss

"After I signed to play baseball professionally, Coach and his family came to watch me pitch in numerous places across the country, from Class A ball to the major leagues. Years later, after I had retired from playing, Coach showed up at my house and we spent an hour reminiscing about baseball and the times we had shared."
- Dan Smith, Jr., GHS Class of 1993

The Crespino household was abuzz with activity as the summer of 2006 approached. A family vacation to the Dominican Republic with Glenna's siblings and their families was scheduled for June. Erica was preparing for her first audiology clinical, a summer experience through Wichita State that preceded her senior year of college. Anthony was looking forward to starting at Pittsburg State in the fall, and his parents were excited about watching him play in the band during PSU football games. Craig and Glenna would be celebrating 25 years of marriage in January, and they were already beginning to discuss plans to do something special for the occasion.

Professionally, Craig was looking forward to a couple of football projects he had in the works. At the annual Girard Alumni Golf Tournament—one of Craig's pet projects—Bill McDonald, a Girard alumnus and baseball coach in the Kansas City area, presented to Craig the idea of updating the GHS weight room. Craig and Bill had met early in Craig's career and become good friends. The two men excitedly imagined what they could accomplish with a little fundraising.

Several years earlier, in 1993, Craig had organized the GHS Strength and Conditioning Meet. Students from throughout the area were invited to compete. The meet, which was held in the GHS weight room, quickly became an annual event, and the number of participants rose every year. Attendance was now nearing 200 student athletes, and Craig was excited about updating the weight room to accommodate the meet, as well as creating a truly special facility that would provide additional motivation for Girard's student athletes. The men set out to raise $25,000 to renovate and improve the space, and the 2006 Girard Alumni Golf Tournament would be the beginning of that fundraising.

Craig was also anxiously awaiting a shipment of new uniforms that he had convinced the administration to purchase for the football team. The devoted coach had spent many hours choosing the perfect look for his beloved Trojans, and he was like a child at Christmas anticipating the arrival of the upcoming delivery. Craig had a special feeling about this year's team. They were a talented bunch, and he had high expectations for them.

Before long, the Crespinos were packing for their trip to the Dominican Republic. The getaway had been planned as a bit of an escape. A deep sadness had settled over Glenna since her mother's death in 2004. Craig and the kids hoped an adventure with family would be a source of healing for her. It had been a long time since the Clark family had spent time away together, and, in fact, the extended family had never done anything quite as extravagant and exhilarating as a week in a tropical paradise.

The morning the Crespinos were to leave for the airport, Becky Martino, Craig and Glenna's friend and neighbor, came over, distressed. Her elderly dog Penny had crawled under the house and refused to come out.

"I'm just so worried because she hasn't been well," Becky began. "What if she's gone under there to die?" The woman's eyes began to fill with tears.

Always willing to help, Craig offered to crawl under the house to retrieve the aging animal.

"I'm a little nervous about getting too close to wiring that may be exposed under there," he confided to Glenna as he changed into something more suitable for the unsavory task. Craig held up his thumb and waggled the digit which still had no fingernail from his last encounter with a live wire. It was not an experience he wished to repeat.

"Well, take a flashlight and be careful," Glenna said, uneasy. She knew he was going to help regardless.

In short order, Craig wriggled into the cramped space and

brought the wary animal out with him. Glenna gave a sigh of relief when he emerged unharmed with the safe, albeit dirty, creature in tow. The grateful neighbor hugged Craig, thanked him for his help, and then wished the Crespinos a wonderful trip before taking her little dog in for a bath.

Glenna smiled at Craig, the hero. She felt incredibly blessed to have such a kind and compassionate husband and couldn't wait for their time away together.

The Dominican Republic was everything they had hoped for. Warm tropical breezes, crystal clear turquoise water, decadent meals, and a laid-back mood that was just what the family needed. Not surprisingly, Craig and Anthony brought a football along and enjoyed playing catch on the beach. One afternoon several locals joined in, and before long they had enough players to divide into teams and play a game. Craig was in his element. He tucked the ball under his arm and ran the distance for a touchdown. The good-natured locals picked him up and threw him into the ocean while his family looked on and laughed. They marveled at Craig's ability to make friends anywhere.

"I wish we could stay forever," Glenna mused as she laid her head on Craig's shoulder later that evening. The two sat at the water's edge waiting for sunset. Not far away, they noticed a couple getting married on the beach.

"Maybe we should renew our vows while we're here," Craig suggested. "Or . . . we could do that for our 25th anniversary in January. What do you think?"

Craig and Glenna discussed the idea as they watched the tropical sky transform into a vivid mingling of warm, vibrant hues. Ultimately, they decided to wait for their anniversary and renew their vows in a church, where their union had begun.

"I just hope I get a ring," Glenna giggled.

It had been almost 20 years since she'd lost her wedding ring, and she had long since gotten used to not having one. Still, Craig had always promised her a new ring, and she was not going to miss an opportunity to tease him about it.

When the Crespinos returned home, the busyness of life returned as well. Erica's summer clinical was scheduled to start soon and she needed to get back to Wichita. Her parents helped her pack her belongings, and then Glenna and her daughter made the drive west together.

Glenna spent three days in Wichita helping Erica unpack and get settled. Craig and Glenna would talk on the phone each evening, sharing stories from their day. Before hanging up, Craig would chat with Erica as well. During one particular call, Craig shared a secret with his daughter.

"I bought your mom a ring! I'm going to give it to her on our anniversary in January! But I want it to be a surprise when we renew our vows, so you have to keep it a secret." The news was practically bursting out of Craig, and he simply had to share it with someone.

"That's awesome, Dad! I can't wait to see it!" Erica smiled furtively, not wanting to spoil the secret with an overly enthusiastic reaction. She knew how much the ring would mean to her mother.

When Glenna returned from Wichita, the Crespino house was quiet. Anthony was at work and Craig was helping a friend paint his house. He painted houses every summer as a way to make a little extra money, which would be particularly helpful now that the Crespinos would have two kids in college. Glenna carried in her suitcase and was heading toward the couple's bedroom to unpack when she noticed a small package on the kitchen counter.

"This is for you," read the sticky note attached to the top of the box. Glenna opened the box to find a beautiful diamond ring. She was stunned, but elated! She put on the ring and immediately got back into her car and drove to where Craig was painting. As Glenna pulled up, Craig realized she'd discovered the surprise and began to laugh.

"Thank you!" Glenna exclaimed, as she ran toward her husband. The two hugged long and tight.

"I love it! And I love you!"

Craig beamed, knowing he'd genuinely surprised her.

"Why didn't you save it for our anniversary?" Glenna was thrilled with the gift but still curious.

"I don't know," Craig began, unsure. "I just felt like I needed to give it to you now."

Glenna smiled. His reasoning didn't matter. She was overjoyed to have a wedding ring again.

Soon it was mid-July, and the Crespinos were already preparing for the upcoming school year. Craig had recently hired Glenna's nephew, Joseph Clark, to help coach football that season. Joseph had transferred from Frontenac to Girard High School his junior year in order to play for his uncle. Coaching with Craig had always been a dream of his, and, having just graduated from college with a degree in education, he had a chance this football season to make that dream a reality. The entire Clark family was thrilled at the idea of Craig and Joseph coaching together.

Craig and Glenna never lost their appreciation for family. Those relationships were treasured above all else. Joseph had recently gotten married, and the couple had purchased a home in Girard, just a few blocks from Craig and Glenna. The Crespinos were very close to Joseph and his new wife, Meredith. Craig had participated in the couple's wedding by reading their chosen scriptures during the Mass, and he and Glenna spent the evening dancing and celebrating. It was a very special day and cherished time together as a family.

Days later, the long-anticipated shipment of new football uniforms arrived at the district board office. When Craig got the call, he could already picture his team running out onto the field in them for the first time. The boys were going to look first class and feel so proud. The 2006 Trojan football season was going to be a great one. Craig smiled at the thought.

As summer break neared its end, Craig and Glenna made plans to go to Wichita to spend the weekend of July 21-23 with Erica before the fall semester began and football season consumed the Crespino household once again. Because of her summer clinical, Erica had not spent the summer at home in Girard as she had in years past. Moments of family togetherness were proving to be all too fleeting now that Erica and Anthony were grown and pursuing their own paths. Craig and Glenna were looking forward to spending time with their daughter and were excited for their weekend getaway.

Anthony was working his summer job at Evans Motors that Friday morning, detailing cars. He occasionally joined his parents for trips to Wichita, but this weekend he had plans to attend a concert in Kansas City with friends. Anthony had driven Craig's car to work that day, but not willingly. Early that morning, Craig had informed his son that he needed his truck to haul some equipment to the high school practice football field in preparation for next week's football camp. Anthony was angry with his father for commandeering his truck when he had plans. He did not want to take his dad's car to the concert. The two had argued about the arrangement, exchanging heated words.

After Anthony left for work, Craig and Glenna made final plans for their road trip to Wichita.

"I've got to go make sure everything is ready for camp first," Craig told Glenna as the two discussed what time to leave.

"I'm having coffee with the girls. Let's try to be on the road by 12:30," Glenna suggested. "I'll let Anthony know."

Craig nodded in agreement, and then made a quick call to 16-year-old student trainer Jace Cobb, asking him to meet him in the equipment room in the high school basement. He kissed his wife goodbye and flew out the door at his usual quick pace.

Glenna packed their bags and then headed out the door as well. Since her mother's death, she and a few friends had been meeting for coffee on Friday mornings. It was therapeutic for Glenna, a chance to laugh and just share life for a couple of hours.

July 21, 2006, was just a typical day for the Craig Crespino family. There was nothing in the warm summer air that morning to forewarn them of the cataclysmic and deadly tragedy, now just moments away, that would change their lives forever.

CHAPTER 9

That Fateful Morning

"Craig meant the world to me. He was my best friend and mentor, and he made the world a better place."

- Joseph Clark, Craig and Glenna's nephew; GHS Class of 2001; GHS football coach, 2006-2007

The morning of July 21, 2006, Blaise Bauer was in his pickup truck heading east toward the Missouri Bootheel. He was on his way to his first professional coon hunt with two of his best coonhounds and was hoping to come home a winner. A fierce competitor, Blaise reveled in the various coonhunting competitions, which typically offered enough in prize money to keep his dogs fed and maybe a bit more. Summers afforded a little extra time for Blaise to pursue his competitive outlet. A weekend road trip would be a welcome reprieve from school duties, which never really ended, even in the summer.

Barely out of Girard, Blaise's cell phone rang.

"Hey, buddy!" It was Craig. "We're getting ready for football camp today. You gonna come out and help coach this year?"

Despite the fact that Blaise was now principal and no longer coaching, Craig would call him every summer to invite him to join the coaching ranks during summer football camp. It was mostly a friendly gesture. Craig knew his principal and friend didn't really have the time to help out, even for a week, but he didn't necessarily need the help either. It was simply a chance to reminisce a bit and make an old friend feel good. Deliberate in his thoughtfulness, Craig always took the time to reach out and make others feel valued and appreciated.

Now heading into his sixth year as Girard High School principal, Blaise had long ago left his coaching years behind him. He missed the game of football, but his position as principal was fulfilling in its own way. Blaise's ability to build relationships with the students served him well. At 6'4" and 225 pounds with a tall, athletic frame, he was somewhat imposing and potentially intimidating, but most students agreed he was also fair and approachable.

Still an ardent fan of the game, Blaise smiled at the call. The two men visited for a few minutes before Craig said, "Well, I better get busy. Jace will be here soon to help." The friends wished each other a good weekend and said goodbye.

Student trainer Jace Cobb pulled into the narrow alley on the north side of the high school. A steep ramp plunged downward near the end of the drive, at the bottom of which was the weights and equipment room. Craig was already at work downstairs, which is where Jace found him.

"Hey, Jace!" Coach Crespino's enthusiastic greeting echoed across the concrete room. A tremendous smile overtook his face at the sight of the high school sophomore.

"Hey, Coach!" Jace thoroughly enjoyed time spent with Coach Crespino and admired how perpetually upbeat he was. His positivity inspired Jace to always try to look on the bright side of things.

"How you been?" The question was genuine and heartfelt.

"Can't complain," Jace replied. "Summer's going too fast, as usual."

They both nodded their heads knowingly, exchanging a hearty handshake.

"Looks like you're having a good summer," Jace continued. "I saw a picture on Facebook of you and Glenna dancing at a wedding."

"We danced the night away." Craig's tan face settled into a smile that exuded pure joy. "Took the whole family to the Dominican Republic with Glenna's side this summer, too. It was fantastic. We haven't done anything like that in a long time."

"Sounds awesome, Coach," Jace could see how much the vacation had meant to Craig.

The two spent a few minutes catching up, then set their sights on the work ahead of them. Coach Crespino knew there was plenty to do that morning, and he had to be home and ready to go to Wichita by 12:30.

Craig and Jace loaded Anthony's truck with equipment and then hopped into the cab and headed toward the team's practice field. It was shaping up to be a typical summer day in southeast Kansas, hot and humid. Summer highs top out around 100°, and humidity levels are often not far behind. Late July means suffocating heat, but the GHS summer football camp was to start in just three days, and Coach Crespino was not about to let the heat slow him down.

In 2006, football camp was the closest thing to practice that Kansas coaches were allowed during the summer break, and they took it seriously. It was their first opportunity to get their entire team on a football field since the previous season ended nearly eight months prior. The Girard Trojan Summer Football Camp always took place during the last full week of July. You could schedule a family vacation around it, and parents appreciated that. But for Coach Crespino, it was strategically planned during the last week allowed by the Kansas State High School Activities Association so that fundamentals, assignments, and plays were fresh in the players' minds when football practice began just two short weeks later.

Craig and Jace pulled up to the practice field and came to a stop in the grass. The Girard High School practice football field is just that, a field. If not for a small equipment shed and a mobile goal post, there is very little to divulge its true identity. Several blocks west of the high school campus, the field hides peacefully behind the local nursing home. The two dead-end roads immediately north and south of the care facility empty into its grassy edges. Two 60-yard gridirons, each running east and west, one just north of the other, serve as practice fields for the team. Beyond the grids to the west is grass, unmowed and wild. A scant tree line on the far west end and another to the north provide natural boundaries for the modest property.

On this sunny Friday morning, Coach Crespino and his

student trainer Jace would transform the unassuming field into a place where teenage warriors would prepare for battle. A recent coaches' poll had the Trojans picked to finish fourth in the nine-team league that year, but Coach Crespino was eager to prove that they would be better than that. He had a strong group of starters returning—and some talented underclassmen as well, new uniforms for his team, and high expectations for the upcoming season.

After 22 years of coaching the Girard Trojans, Coach Craig Crespino *was* Girard football. He had accrued five league titles in his fourteen years as head coach, and his gregarious personality ensured that anyone who knew anything about high school football in southeast Kansas knew Craig Crespino.

Together the coach and trainer unloaded equipment from the truck, placing some of the items in the small storage shed on the east end of the practice field. As they worked, they chatted about the upcoming season, the weather, the usual things. When the last few items had been unloaded and put in place, Craig locked the shed door and then raised and latched the truck's tailgate. He was almost done for the morning. It was getting close to noon, and he was eager to hit the road with Glenna to go see Erica.

"All right, last item on the list." Craig motioned toward the mobile goal post sitting beyond the two marked practice grids. "Let's get that baby moved into place!"

Craig was already walking briskly in that direction as Jace turned to look at the object. The student trainer nodded dutifully and took off after the coach across the field.

Only one goal post was needed for practice or camp; it

would stand at the west end of the north field. Craig and Jace each grabbed a leg of the H-shaped apparatus and began dragging it toward its customary position. Although large and cumbersome, the metal goal post was portable, and GHS coaches and players had moved it around the field for years. It had a slightly different resting place with each summer mowing and only settled in the end zone of the north field when the team's season was about to begin.

Moving the goal post into position was just an ordinary task for the two, during an ordinary conversation, on an ordinary day. Until it wasn't.

CHAPTER 10

The Accident

"Growing up without a father, it meant a lot that a man like Coach Crespino would randomly stop by my house just to talk to me. I now know the importance of taking time to chat and give encouraging words and love to others, specifically those in tough situations."
- Johnny Webb, GHS Class of 2009

Craig and Jace chatted as they moved the hefty goal post across the practice football field. Silence was fleeting when Coach Craig Crespino was around. Jace appreciated Coach's innate gift of communication and truly relished their time together. An ardent conversationalist, Craig was in the middle of a sentence when suddenly a fierce jolt threw Jace backward and to the ground.

Stunned and dazed, the student trainer opened his eyes and saw nothing but sky. His whole body felt stiff and sore.

Unsure of what had happened, Jace looked around for Coach. He was horrified by what he saw. Coach Crespino lay lifeless on the ground. For the first time since Jace had known him, Coach was not moving.

Jace's eyes traveled up the tall, metal goal post, and he realized that the upright to which Coach Crespino still clung had come in contact with an overhead power line. A lethal measure of electricity had surged through the post seeking the ground. Jace had been thrown back by the deadly current, but Craig's body had become part of its path. His muscles contracted around the pole and he was unable to let go, even as the remorseless current continued to flow.

Jace made his way back to Anthony's truck for his cell phone. He had to get help for Coach Crespino! He grabbed his phone off the dash and dialed 911.

"Hello?" Jace stammered, still foggy. "We need help at the practice football field!"

Jace did his best to inform the operator of the dire situation.

Within a few terrible minutes, the peaceful tranquility of the quiet, rural town was shattered by the ominous noise of sirens coming from every direction—a disturbingly foreign sound in a small community where everyone knows everyone. Hearts lurched as residents took inventory of loved ones and then said a quick and fervent prayer for the unfortunate soul awaiting the wailing vehicles.

Police Chief Jeff McDonald was the first to arrive at the practice field. Officer McDonald had just recently been promoted to chief of police after spending the previous four years as the school resource officer for the Girard school district.

During his time as SRO, he had worked closely with Craig Crespino and was devastated by what he saw as he pulled onto the scene. He positioned his squad car to obscure the terrible sight before him and then moved Jace to an area behind his car.

Additional emergency personnel soon arrived and extended the barrier with their vehicles to prevent onlookers from witnessing the tragedy. A frantic call was made to the city to shut off the power. EMS responder Brandon Myers tended to Jace and helped him to an ambulance. Although Jace did not have any visible wounds, he was taken to nearby Girard Medical Center by ambulance for a thorough examination.

The first responders very quickly realized the gravity of Coach Crespino's injuries and the need for Crawford County Coroner, Dr. Adam Paoni. They called it in.

Dr. Paoni and his son Ben were at Evans Motors shopping for a vehicle. It was Ben's 16th birthday, and he was excited to be getting a car. The father-son duo had just returned to the lot after taking a vehicle for a test drive. As the two visited with the friendly salesmen, they heard the sirens and watched as one emergency vehicle after another whizzed past the Girard car dealership. The sheer number of vehicles told Adam he would be getting a call soon.

"Well, fellas, this may have to wait," the doctor told the men. Adam and Ben said their goodbyes and headed for home. Almost immediately, Adam's cell phone rang. It was dispatch.

"We've got a fatality at the high school practice field," the caller reported.

"What happened?" Adam inquired, alarmed but also confused as to how anyone could be killed in the open field behind the nursing home.

"Possible electrocution." She paused before adding, "It might be Craig Crespino."

Adam's heart sank. The Paonis were close friends of the Crespinos. Adam considered Craig to be one of his best friends, and his wife Faith was having coffee with Glenna Crespino at that very moment. High school junior Ben Paoni had worked side by side with Craig painting houses every summer since his eighth-grade year and was excited to be playing football for his good friend that fall. Craig had called Ben earlier that week hoping he would be available to help get the field ready for football camp that Friday morning, but Ben had declined because of his family's plans for his birthday. As they rushed home, Adam and Ben prayed that somehow the report was wrong—that their dear friend Craig had not just died on Ben's birthday.

In the back lot of Evans Motors, Anthony Crespino was also hearing the sirens. He went about his work for the day, thinking little of the commotion. Soon, however, the car lot owner came out of the office and approached him.

"Anthony, I just got a phone call that there's been an accident at the practice field. I don't really know any details," the man told Anthony. "But you might want to go over there and see what's going on."

Anthony became extremely worried. Suddenly the multitude of sirens hit home, and he jumped in his dad's vehicle and hurried to the field. He pulled in on the south end, farthest from the scene, expecting to see a lawnmower accident. His dad was always out there tending to the field and had borrowed his truck that morning to move what Anthony assumed was probably mowing equipment. Instead, he saw a wall of flashing emergency vehicles and a frenzy of first responders at work.

Anthony started off toward the chaos when one of Craig's former players appeared and gave him a huge, emotional hug.

"I'm so sorry, man!" The distraught young man hugged Anthony tight.

Startled and now frantic, Anthony's mind raced, and he wondered what in the world could have brought on this bizarre encounter. Before he could ask, Glenna's brother Joe Clark pulled up. Joe had been at his son Joseph's house mowing the lawn while Joseph and new wife Meredith were away on their honeymoon. Somehow, Joe had gotten word of the accident and had immediately headed to the field, where he found Anthony trying to make his way to the scene. He coaxed his nephew back to his truck where he gave him the devastating news. Joe then drove Anthony home.

The Crespino house was already filling with people who had heard rumors of an accident involving Craig. Anthony quickly retreated to his room to be alone. It was all too overwhelming. He sat on his bed and recalled his last words to his dad. They were not kind. A deep sense of regret collided with the gut-wrenching grief that enveloped him.

Adam Paoni's drive to the practice field was a blur. He first dropped Ben off at their home, which was a block from the field, then rushed to the scene. Jumping out of his car, he ran toward the crowd. Assistant Fire Chief Dustin Johnson met him as he neared the line of emergency vehicles.

"Is it Craig?" Adam practically screamed.

"I don't know, Adam. I just got here myself. Let me go find out."

The devastated doctor walked in nervous circles, praying fervently as he waited for the firefighter to return.

Dustin's head hung low as he returned with the terrible news. "It's Craig."

Adam dropped to his knees and cradled his head in his hands.

"I can't do this," he told Dustin, tears welling in his eyes. "I don't want to see him like that."

The somber firefighter nodded sympathetically and put his hand on Adam's shoulder.

"We'll have them call Joey," referring to Crawford County EMS Director Joey Adams.

Adam lingered in disbelief, utterly heartbroken. He pulled his phone out of his pocket and called his wife, Faith. Aware that she was with Glenna at that moment, he gave her few details and tried to remain calm. He asked her to come to the field immediately, and then put the phone back in his pocket and folded in a heap in the grass.

"Dammit, Craig!" he muttered to himself. "Always in a hurry."

For as long as Adam had known Craig, he knew Craig to have only one speed—fast. He walked fast, talked fast, drove fast. He was a ball of energy and was always rushing to the next thing on his schedule, sometimes with reckless abandon.

Minutes later, Adam heard a car racing into the north

parking area at the edge of the field. He looked up to see the vehicle lurch to a hurried stop, and his wife Faith furiously exit the car. He pulled himself to standing, gathered his strength, and went to meet her.

As Adam shared the terrible news with Faith, he caught sight of someone on foot, running to the accident scene from the south end of the field.

"Oh God. No!" Adam yelled, and he took off running toward the frantic woman.

It was Glenna.

CHAPTER 11

A Family's Worst Nightmare

"He lived life to the fullest through friends, players, coaches, and especially family. God gives us people like Craig to enjoy, and for everyone he touched, that was easy!"

- Coach Dennis Franchione, Glenna's uncle; former head coach for Pittsburg State University, New Mexico State, Texas Christian University, University of Alabama, Texas A&M, and Texas State

Glenna Crespino was spending her morning with friends Faith Paoni, Michelle McFarland, and Bobbi Mahnken. As the ladies enjoyed their Friday morning coffee at Michelle's flower shop on the square, the sound of sirens drifted in and out of their conversation, but they gave them little thought.

Just before noon the shop phone rang. Michelle answered

it, and Glenna sensed immediately that something was wrong. She could not make out most of the conversation but did manage to catch the phrase "accident on the practice field."

"An accident at the practice field? I think that's where Craig is this morning," she said nervously as she reached for her phone and dialed Craig's number.

As Glenna waited for her husband to answer, Faith's phone rang.

"Faith, I need you." Faith could sense a terrible urgency in her husband's voice. "The children are fine. I need you to get down to the practice field. It's bad."

Faith's heart raced as she absorbed the message, but she gave no indication to her friends in order not to alarm them. She informed the group that she had to go. Desperate to get there before Glenna, Faith began digging feverishly for her keys.

Despite Faith's attempts to avoid a panic, when Craig did not answer his phone Glenna ran out the back door of the shop. The Crespino home was only two blocks away and Glenna had walked to the shop that morning for coffee.

"Stop her!" Faith yelled to Michelle. She looked at Bobbi and said, "Come with me!" The two women raced to Faith's car and took off for the practice field.

As Glenna ran toward her house for her car, an overwhelming sense of dread overtook her. She recalled conversations that she and Craig had had about the need for a phone at the practice field in case a student was hurt. When Craig began carrying a cell phone, those concerns were alleviated a bit. But this did little to ease Glenna's anxiety at the moment, as she imagined all the worst possible scenarios.

Before Glenna could reach her vehicle on foot, Michelle pulled up beside her.

"Glenna, get in!" Michelle insisted. "I'll drive you there!"

Glenna was in a total panic by this time, and her friend absolutely could not move fast enough for her. Every second that passed was excruciating. She closed her eyes and clenched her fists as she willed Michelle to move faster and get her to that field.

Faith and Bobbi arrived at the north edge of the practice field and frantically got out of the car. A profusion of emergency vehicles concealed any hint of what had taken place. Faith spotted Adam and headed toward him, while Bobbi ran to the south drive when she saw Michelle pull up with Glenna.

Glenna jumped out of the car and began running toward the northwest corner of the field. It was a blur of flashing lights, chaos, and despair, and everything in her sensed the gravity of the situation. A policeman met her en route, stopping her from reaching the scene of the accident.

"My husband is over there!" Glenna cried desperately, trying to push past him.

"You can't go there right now," the officer said, sympathetic but steadfast. "Craig's been in an accident."

"Oh God! Please let me go to him!" Glenna pleaded, but the answer remained the same. Now out of her mind with worry, she looked around and saw Adam Paoni running toward her.

"Adam!" Glenna ran to him, hoping that perhaps her good friend could help. "You have to let me see him! *Please*!"

Adam placed his hands firmly on Glenna's shoulders.

"You can't, Glenna," he strained, out of breath and distraught. "It's bad. Craig's gone."

"No!" screamed Glenna. "No, he's not! Get over there and help him!"

Adam withered in despair. "It's true, Glenna. I'm so sorry!"

Glenna's brother Joe had returned to the field after taking Anthony home. He ran to his sister and held her tight. Faith, Michelle and Bobbi were also trying to console Glenna when Michelle's cell phone rang. It was her husband Mark, who had just learned of the accident during a summer class he was taking at PSU. Another student in the class, a cousin of Glenna's, had shared the news with Mark and had also called her stepbrother in Texas. Glenna became hysterical.

"If someone in *Texas* knows, then it could get to Erica and Anthony before I can tell them!" Glenna's heart hammered in her chest as she felt the extreme urgency to get to her children.

Joe tried to calm his sister. "I've already told Anthony. He's at home. Mike is there. Erin and Dylan are with him, too. Let's just figure out how to get ahold of Erica." Glenna's youngest brother Mike had rushed to the Crespino home along with his son Dylan when he had learned of the accident. Anthony's friend Erin had done the same.

"I can't just call Erica and give her this news!" Glenna sobbed. "I want to be the one to tell her, but someone has to be with her. I don't want her to be alone—and I don't want her to drive here by herself, which is what she'll try to do!" Glenna knew Erica would want to get to her family immediately. The thought of her daughter making the long drive from Wichita while frantic with grief was more than Glenna could bear.

After reaching out unsuccessfully to a couple of friends in Wichita, Glenna was able to get in touch with John and Beth Kotzman's daughter, Kelli Janzen, who also lived there and would go to Erica. Glenna asked Kelli not to give Erica the news; she wanted that to come from her.

With Anthony at home and a friend on her way to Erica, Glenna surrendered her attempts to see Craig and agreed to leave the field and return to the house. She went directly to Anthony's room, where she found him surrounded by friends and family. The mother and son clung to each other in utter despair.

In Wichita, Erica had just arrived at her summer job and was getting ready for the day's appointments. She noticed that she had missed several calls from friends in Girard but decided whatever it was could wait until after work. Almost immediately, however, Erica spotted her longtime friend Kelli walking into the facility. Erica could tell Kelli had been crying and was visibly shaken.

"We need to go outside and talk," Kelli told Erica.

"What is it?" Erica asked, concerned. The two friends left the building as Erica urged Kelli to tell her what was going on.

"You need to call home," Kelli said, honoring Glenna's request that she be the one to give Erica the devastating news.

Erica could sense something was terribly wrong. She was expecting her parents for a visit later that afternoon and could not imagine what might be so urgent that the news couldn't wait until they arrived. She called their home phone and got a strange voice on the other end.

"Hi, this is Erica. Who's this?"

"Oh, Erica! This is Michelle," came the anguished reply. "I'm going to put your mom on."

"Wait! What's going on?" Erica demanded frantically, but there was no response as Michelle quickly handed the phone off.

Glenna's voice trembled as she told Erica of the tragic accident. Erica could hardly breathe as she listened to her mother's words. It couldn't be true. It just simply couldn't be true! They were coming to see her that afternoon. It had to be a terrible mistake! Erica fell into a fog of despair.

Eventually, Kelli gathered Erica into her car, and the two friends headed toward Girard. The drive from Wichita was a dreadful blur of phone calls and tears for the distraught young women. Glenna was extremely worried about Kelli and Erica making the two-and-a-half-hour drive while emotionally distracted. After fretting for more than an hour, Glenna asked Joe to drive her west toward Wichita to meet the girls. Two hours into their journey, Kelli pulled over outside of the small town of St. Paul, Kansas, where Glenna and Joe had just arrived and were waiting for them.

Once Erica saw her devastated mother, the awful news sunk in and became real. Glenna and Erica stood on the side of the road and held each other. In one dreadful instant their entire world had been turned upside down. Life as they knew it had ended. Nothing would ever be the same again.

Erica got into the car with her mother and uncle and rode the remainder of the drive with them while Kelli followed. They pulled up to their home to find the yard full of people and what seemed like a hundred cars surrounding the house. Despite the buzz of activity, a heavy sense of sorrow and despair made the once cheerful home feel empty and lonely.

With both her children now home, Glenna's thoughts turned to Craig's parents, Frank and JoAnn. Again, Glenna went to her brother Joe. After losing her father at such a young age, Glenna thought of Joe as a father figure and had always depended on him a great deal.

"Can you please go to Frank and JoAnn and give them the news?"

Joe immediately agreed. He got in his truck and drove to the elder Crespinos' home in Pittsburg. He knocked on their door, his heart heavier than he ever knew it could be. Frank answered the door. His wife JoAnn was at work, and he had been doing some housecleaning.

"Hi, Joe!" Frank was surprised to see him. "What's up?"

Joe gently ushered Frank into the living room and had him sit down.

"I'm so sorry to tell you this, Frank, but Craig has been in an accident, and he's gone."

Frank sank back into the couple's couch as Joe relayed to him the awful details of the accident.

"I was running the sweeper earlier today," Frank told Joe. "The cord shot out a spark, and just like that it quit working. I guess that was Craig saying goodbye."

Joe put his hand on Frank's shoulder. The two men hung their heads in deep sadness. When Frank had collected himself, they made their way to Joe's truck to go to JoAnn's workplace and give her the news. They called for an ambulance, unsure of what her reaction might be. A police officer met them there as well, and together they gave Craig's mother the worst news of her life.

JoAnn was inconsolable.

"It should have been me!" she sobbed repeatedly.

Joe drove the Crespinos back to their home where they called Craig's brother Curt in Kansas City. Frank and JoAnn waited for Curt to make the drive down, and then the three drove together to Girard, where they found Craig and Glenna's house full of friends and family.

The Paonis were among those who had gathered to support the Crespino family. Because Dr. Paoni was the county coroner, Erica begged him to let her see her dad. To hold his hand one last time. She vividly remembered the lines in his hands and how they felt in hers. She desperately wanted to have one more opportunity to memorize those hands and treasure their feel. To hold them with the unbearable understanding that this final touch would have to last her a lifetime. But Adam assured her that she did not want to see her father's wounded body. He urged Erica to remember him as she last saw him—joyful, smiling, full of life. She reluctantly conceded.

Erica turned her focus to being strong for her family. She felt it was now up to her to hold them together. Although just 21 years old, she was compelled to take on the role that Craig had played in the family. She and her dad were so much alike. Stubborn and hardheaded. Determined and driven. Outgoing and friendly. Never knowing a stranger. Glenna and Anthony were more introverted. Erica worried about their emotional well-being. She tried to conceal her grief and be strong for her mother and brother, but inside she was completely heartbroken.

Glenna sat among the crowd of friends and family who were busy cleaning, cooking, and consoling. She was trying hopelessly to wish it all away. She knew in her heart that she would have to succumb and accept this horrible new reality. She looked down at her new wedding ring and squeezed it tight with her right hand. Two weeks. She had worn it for *two weeks*.

CHAPTER 12

The Aftermath

*"I remember Coach would end every practice
by telling us, 'Gentlemen, go home and tell your
mom and dad you love them because you never
know what tomorrow will bring.'"*
- Ben Paoni, GHS Class of 2008

Blaise's leisurely road trip took him eastward into neighboring Missouri. It was a familiar drive and one he had made many times on his way to his hometown of Monett. He savored a hunting road trip, particularly when he was by himself. The life of a principal was often chaotic and always busy; the solitude would be a welcome change for a few days.

Around 1 p.m. Blaise's cell phone rang. The phone's display said "DAN DULING," the principal of Girard's R.V. Haderlein Elementary.

"Hey, Blaise," Dan started cautiously. "Have you heard anything about an accident in Girard?"

"No, I haven't. What're you talking about?" Blaise asked nervously.

"I heard there was an accident at the practice football field. I think Craig Crespino was involved . . . and a student . . . and I'm hearing there was a fatality."

"Oh, no!" Blaise's heart sank into his stomach.

"I don't know much else right now," Dan continued. "But if I hear anything, I'll let you know."

"Yes, please do," Blaise sighed, utterly sickened at what he had just heard.

The trusty pickup came to a stop at the side of the road. There would be no coon hunt for its occupants tonight. With a heavy heart, Blaise tried to process the news that either his good friend was dead or one of their high school students was. Either scenario was positively dreadful, and he couldn't bear to speculate as to what had happened.

He didn't have to.

Within minutes, his cell phone rang again.

"CRAIG CRESPINO," the phone display reported.

Oh, man, Blaise thought. *We lost a student. Craig is going to be devastated.*

"Hello," Blaise answered solemnly, expecting to hear Craig's very distraught voice on the other end.

Instead, it was a woman's voice. Distraught, yes. But Craig, no.

It was Crespino family friend, Michelle McFarland. She was at the scene and had used Craig's cell phone to access Blaise's mobile number. Time seemed eerily suspended as the caller conveyed what she knew of the unimaginable tragedy. Blaise could scarcely believe what he was hearing. He had just talked to Craig that morning. It was surreal. He struggled to absorb the news that his larger-than-life friend and colleague was dead.

Suddenly, the whole world had changed. In light of the absolutely horrific news, the only thing that mattered now was getting back to Girard and being with the Crespino family and the rest of the Girard community. Blaise turned his truck around and hastily headed west. As he drove toward home, his cell phone rang continuously. Word of the accident was spreading through the small town like a catastrophic brush fire. Stunned residents were in disbelief, completely upended by shock and sorrow.

In between calls, Blaise prayed for the Crespino family. He was heartsick for Glenna, Erica, and Anthony. He could only imagine the agony they were experiencing at that moment. He worried about Glenna's emotional state, knowing how she and Craig treasured family above all else. The idea of Glenna without Craig was heartbreaking to him. He thought about Erica and Anthony and imagined the anguish of losing one's father so suddenly. And what of Craig's parents, Frank and JoAnn? How terrible to lose a child—at any age. It was all so tragic and awful. He desperately wanted to be able to ease the family's suffering, but realized that was an impossible wish.

Blaise also thought about how Craig's death would impact GHS students and staff members. They would all need time to grieve and heal, but there was no time. Football camp was to start in three days, practice in two weeks, and school in just three weeks.

Contemplating what he would need to do as principal to prepare for the upcoming school year was not what Blaise wanted to be thinking about. Unfortunately, he would not have the luxury of taking time to grieve his friend. He had to figure out what to do about the GHS football camp that was scheduled to start on Monday and determine who would teach Craig's classes when school resumed in three short weeks. He had to prepare to address the faculty about the tragic loss of their friend and colleague and ensure that adequate counseling services were available for students. He would have to meet with the assistant football coaches about the upcoming season and gather the team to reassure them that he would do whatever was necessary for them to have the best season possible under the awful circumstances. It was overwhelming.

Tyler Bennett was mowing his family's yard that hot summer afternoon. The high school junior had been the JV quarterback the previous football season. With the varsity quarterback recently graduated, Tyler was expected to step in as the varsity QB this season. The athletic standout was excited for the opportunity.

The July heat was brutal that day, so Tyler took a break from mowing and ran into the house to grab a glass of water. He quickly checked his phone as well and noticed he'd missed a call from his good friend and teammate Ben Paoni. Tyler returned the call immediately, expecting an invitation to go fishing later that day. Instead, he was blindsided by the words, "Coach is dead."

In a fog of disbelief, Tyler left the mower in the yard and drove to Ben's house. He wasn't even sure why; he just needed to be with someone else who was feeling his pain at that moment. The terrible yoke of grief and helplessness required more than one set of shoulders for both young men. They sat together and shared the burden of the tragic news, ultimately knowing they had to go to Coach's house.

The young men pulled up to the Crespino home to find the yard full of people, mostly students. The red, swollen eyes of their peers told a story of unbearable heartache. Many of their teammates were already there, wanting to support the family, but also looking to be comforted.

Junior lineman Tyler Edwards pulled up shortly after Ben and Tyler. He had heard the news while having lunch in a Pittsburg restaurant and had rushed back to Girard. He tried to tell himself that there had to be a mistake, that it couldn't possibly be true. But once he saw the crowd and the number of cars, he knew. He joined the other players in the yard.

The teammates gathered, desperate for consolation. Just that morning, they were anxiously looking forward to their football camp that was to start Monday. Now, football was the last thing on their minds. Coach Crespino was more than just their coach; he was their friend, their mentor, their advocate, and their biggest and loudest cheerleader.

A few at a time, the young men went into the house, which was also full of people. It was uncomfortable and awkward. They were hopelessly unsure of what to say to the Crespino family at such a terrible time. Glenna hugged them graciously and thanked them for being there. She assured them how much they meant to Craig.

Glenna looked at senior running back Mike Cook and said, "Craig just asked me a couple days ago if you could move in with us." Mike had been staying with extended family until the situation had recently become complicated. She hugged the young man, who was clearly suffering from the loss. "He genuinely believed in you, Mike."

That was Craig, willing to do whatever was necessary to help "his kids."

Later that evening Tyler Bennett, Tyler Edwards, Ben Paoni, and a handful of other friends and teammates gathered in the Bennetts' basement. They sat in a circle and told stories about Coach Crespino. They laughed and cried.

"You could call Coach anytime, day or night, and he'd be there to talk to you," one of them recollected.

"He was like a second father to all of us."

A wave of nodding heads indicated they had all experienced that closeness with Coach Crespino. The young men talked late into the night, their feelings of loss and sadness relieved only by the sense of being together.

Meanwhile, Glenna, Erica and Anthony spent that night at Glenna's brother's house in Frontenac. They could not bring themselves to sleep in their home without Craig. The three discussed funeral arrangements, among other things that they never imagined they would be discussing a mere 24 hours earlier. It seemed impossible that their lives had taken such a cruel and dramatic turn in just a matter of hours.

Words cannot adequately describe the impact the terrible accident had on the Crespino family. The suddenness, the unexpectedness, the complete horror of the accident. We don't prepare for something like that. We can't. On the contrary, we spend our years carefully knitting together the fibers of our lives, blissfully ignoring the fact that one ruthless tug can unravel our beautiful tapestry into a tangled web of wreck-age. Craig's death had left the Crespinos hopelessly stranded in the dreadful wreckage that was once their gloriously perfect existence.

CHAPTER 13

A Community Mourns

"Craig was the quintessential coach. He loved the game and he loved the players."
- John Kotzman, Crespino family friend; GHS head football coach, 1977-1991

All of southeast Kansas lost a friend and advocate that terrible July day. It was a vicious lesson on the utter fragility of life, and it hit residents of the area like a violent Kansas squall, leaving destruction and heartache in its wake. High school football fans across the area had been anxiously gearing up for a new season. Now, the news of Coach Craig Crespino's death overshadowed all excitement, and the cruel reality that everything dear can be taken in an instant shackled the populace with sorrow. A stormy cloud of anguished bereavement settled over the entire corner of the rural Midwestern state.

The evening of Monday, July 24, the Girard football team should have been relaxing after their first day of summer football camp with their energetic head coach. Instead, they sat in the stands of their high school stadium attending a rosary service for their fallen leader. More than a thousand people gathered to offer prayers for the beloved coach. The service was held at the Girard High School football field, in part as a tribute to Craig's love of the game but even more so out of sheer necessity, as there was no other venue in town that could hold the enormous crowd.

The family had requested that attendees wear Trojan colors instead of the usual dark funeral garb. A sea of maroon and gold spilled out of the stands and into the surrounding lot. The football team wore their game jerseys and gathered as a group. Jace had been released from the hospital and was able to attend and sit with the team. He had sustained minor injuries to one leg but was incredibly fortunate that he had not suffered serious physical damage. Emotionally, he was coping as well as could be expected and was determined to be there for Glenna and the family. The Crespinos were equally committed to supporting him as well.

It was a difficult but endearing evening for the family. Hundreds and hundreds of people approached them to offer condolences and share stories of how Craig touched their lives. His death transcended the community of Girard and impacted thousands.

As the crowd eventually began to disperse, Blaise noticed a high school student standing by himself, sobbing.

"You okay?" the sympathetic principal asked as he approached him.

The young man shook his head gloomily. "I'm gonna miss 'Pino."

Mr. Bauer smiled at the student's affectionate name for Coach Crespino. He put his hand on the teen's shoulder.

"We all are," he replied sadly.

"Not long ago," the young man began, "I got in trouble at school and was sent home. I was working on my bike in the front yard, and Coach stopped and talked to me for probably half an hour." He wiped his eyes as he continued. "He didn't ask why I was in trouble—he just asked about my bike. I know he didn't really care about that bike. He just cared about me."

That was Craig in a nutshell: genuine, compassionate, kind. To everyone. It didn't matter if you were the starting quarterback or someone with no athletic ability at all. You mattered to Craig. He truly loved "his kids" and did everything he could to support and encourage them. He was determined to see them succeed in high school and beyond.

The following morning—Tuesday, July 25—hundreds of friends and family made their way to Memorial Auditorium in neighboring Pittsburg for the 10 a.m. funeral Mass for Coach Craig Crespino. In anticipation of the large crowd, special permission was granted by the Catholic Church for the Mass to be offered at the auditorium, which seated more than 1,500 people.

For Glenna, Erica, and Anthony, mentally preparing themselves for the funeral was agonizing. Glenna was frail from lack of sleep and an inability to eat. Her brother Joe urged her to have a sports drink so that she didn't become dehydrated. Glenna forced it down.

"I don't know if I can do this," Glenna cried, collapsing

into a chair in the family's living room. The weighty yoke of grief was taking a toll. Family and friends rallied around her. Together they made their way to Pittsburg, into the auditorium, and to the front row.

The spacious venue was filled beyond capacity. The Girard football team sat together wearing their Trojan jerseys, and a group of fellow referees in the balcony wore their black-and-white-striped shirts. People stood shoulder to shoulder along the back and sides. To accommodate possible overflow, the basement of the facility had been set up with chairs and a large screen on which the service was streamed. This additional space was standing room only as well.

The family had requested memorials be made to the GHS weight room renovation project in lieu of flowers. Regardless, a profusion of florals covered the casket and adorned the stage, the likes of which few had ever seen. A Girard Trojan helmet and a football sat atop the casket as well.

The six pallbearers chosen by the family represented the most important aspects of Craig's life. John Black, Adam Paoni and Bryan Cherry were dear friends who had supported Craig throughout the years. John wore his referee shirt in honor of the many games he and Craig had officiated together.

Chuck Smith and Bob Campbell were selected as both friends and fellow coaches. Coach Smith represented Craig's fondness and devotion to St. Mary's Colgan schools as well. Bob Campbell was the head coach at nearby Fort Scott High School. He and Craig had become acquainted through the Southeast Kansas Coaches Association that Craig established. The two became good friends, and Craig later served as best man in Bob's wedding. When the newlyweds had their first child, Craig and Glenna were asked to be godparents.

Denny Peak was a former player under Coach Crespino. He had spent several summers mowing grass with Craig for the school district, and the two became especially close when Denny followed in Craig's footsteps and became a middle and high school football coach. Craig had been a mentor to Denny, and Craig and Glenna were godparents to Denny's son.

The game of football had gifted the Crespinos with many special friendships.

Blaise was asked to read the family's chosen scriptures during the Mass. The Reverend Bob McElwee presided and offered a moving tribute to the loving husband, doting father, spirited coach, and esteemed educator.

"When Craig first started coaching, he wore his father's coaching shoes," the priest recounted. "He wore them during every game, until they were so tattered and worn that they had to be replaced." This simple act beautifully defined the deep respect and admiration Craig had for his father.

He went on to describe Craig's love for his wife Glenna and their children, Erica and Anthony.

"Craig insisted that Glenna sit in the same place at every football game so that he could always look up in the stands and find her. A coach whose wife doesn't feel like she takes a backseat to the beloved game is a man who knows where his priorities lie and is perpetually and purposefully mindful of the importance of his family. Craig's family always knew that they were his first and truest love."

The emotional anguish was more than Glenna could take. Her stomach began to churn and she felt its meager contents wanting to come up. She looked at Erica with an understood sense of panic, and Erica ran for a trash can. She held it under her mother's chin as the little bit of sports drink Glenna had consumed earlier that morning made its way back up. The devastated widow was inconsolable, her cruel circumstances throwing yet another punch at their already fragile victim.

The priest continued, painting a grand portrait of a man who loved his family and friends. Loved the game of football. Loved working with kids. Loved life. Stories that just a week ago were part of what made Girard such a wonderful place to live. Now they were brutal reminders of the gaping void left by the loss of such a special man and of all that the little town had lost in that one terrible moment.

"Craig set out to make those he coached better people, as every coach should. So, let us be coached by Craig and Glenna, seeking a job that is not just a job but rather a vocation and a calling." The sheer number of people in attendance affirmed the truth of Fr. McElwee's words. Craig had touched so many lives in an incredibly positive way.

"There is no way to make sense of the accident that took Craig Crespino's life," the priest concluded. "But be sure that God will bring something good from it."

When the funeral Mass was over, a somber stream of mourners trickled out of the auditorium and made their way to their cars. Crespino family members sat behind the hearse and waited as the casket was placed in the long, black vehicle. The football team and their coaches loaded the school bus which had brought them there as a group and would be delivering them to the cemetery as well. Police officers closed down a multitude of intersections in preparation for the procession of vehicles that would be making the slow, solemn 15-mile drive from Memorial Auditorium in Pittsburg to the Girard Cemetery. Scores of vehicles, stretching on for over a mile, followed the hearse on its final journey that late Tuesday morning.

Family, friends, coworkers, students, former students, classmates and mere acquaintances surrounded the gravesite, grief-stricken and in disbelief. The football team huddled together, arm in arm, their hearts breaking. They lingered after the ceremony, not wanting to leave their fallen leader behind. The assistant coaches gently began moving the players toward the bus. Tyler Bennett turned to leave but heard someone call out his name. He looked to see his high school basketball coach, who had an urgent message for the young quarterback.

With tear-filled eyes the coach forced out the words, "Lead them, Tyler."

The words hit Tyler hard. He suddenly realized the team would be leaning heavily on their quarterback that season. Tyler nodded and boarded the bus. He settled into a seat alongside a teammate and thought about the coach's charge. The 2006 football season would be his first time starting at varsity quarterback, already a tremendous responsibility for a high school junior. This was next-level pressure, but he was ready. The uncertainty of a season without their beloved Coach still loomed large, but a switch had been flipped inside Tyler. His personal grieving time was over. It was time to step up and be the leader this team would need.

The team's bus drove away, and then the remaining vehicles, one by one. Eventually, the Crespino family was at the gravesite alone. The fanfare was over, the crowd was gone, and all they were left with was their grief. It didn't feel right to leave their loved one and go home, but they knew in their hearts that Craig was not there. He was in a better place now, watching over them. They slowly returned to their vehicles and drove home in silence, emotionally depleted.

CHAPTER 14

The Empty Shoes

"Frank Crespino would often be at practices and I always envied Craig's relationship with his father. They were very close and Craig had a deep respect for Frank."
- Dave Wutke, GHS football coach, 1994-2007

Unbearable grief poured out that hot July day, like a tormented river of anguish bursting beyond its banks. It felt like nothing would ever be the same, and in some ways, it wouldn't. Craig Crespino's enthusiasm was the lifeblood of the community. His friendliness to all and his genuine affection and concern for his students were part of what made Girard the idyllic town that residents loved.

The sad fact is, you cannot replace someone like Craig Crespino. Unfortunately, for Craig's longtime friend Blaise, that was precisely the sickening task before him. He had only days to find personnel to teach Craig's classes and assume his many extracurricular duties for the fast-approaching fall semester.

Blaise hoped Glenna's nephew, Joseph Clark, would take the classroom duties. The new teacher had the necessary certification to teach the classes, and Blaise knew the difficult transition would be a bit less painful for the students if someone Craig loved was in that position. Joseph and his new wife Meredith were on their way home from their honeymoon. The couple had cut their trip short after receiving word of the accident. Blaise would approach him when he returned.

Girard High School math teacher and head golf coach, Steve Curran, was asked to assume Craig's athletic director duties, and he readily agreed to help fill that void. Craig's class sponsorship and other duties were also delegated to various staff members.

As building principal, Blaise prepared a statement and a plan of action for the first inservice days with the high school staff. Wanting to remain positive and uplifting, he was ready to present the situation to them as an opportunity to do great things for Girard High School students. He explored the option of having a crisis team and additional counselors available for students during the first few weeks after classes resumed but ultimately decided it was best not to reopen wounds that hopefully would have begun to heal. The school counselor was well prepared to assist any students needing emotional support.

Blaise's final and most difficult dilemma was determining who would fill the role of head football coach. Without a doubt, football had lost its luster for the Girard Trojan players. They could not fathom the idea of a new head coach. No one could replace their beloved Coach Crespino, and frankly, no one wanted to. Yet, in reality, the matter had to be addressed.

Blaise scheduled a meeting with the available coaching staff: Craig Siebert, Dave Wutke, Jeremiah Hudson, and Nick Cheney. Even more so than usual, this dedicated group of men would play a vital role in the upcoming season. Under normal circumstances, high school football coaches spend an enormous amount of time making sure student athletes are physically, academically, and emotionally prepared to compete. They make a great number of sacrifices in order to ensure the well-being and success of their players. Under these dire circumstances, the Trojan coaching staff understood the extraordinary season ahead was going to require even more from them.

Coach Craig Siebert was a 1989 Girard graduate who played high school football under John Kotzman and Craig Crespino. He started coaching with Craig in 1993, the last year that Blaise coached at Girard. He and his wife Tiffany were close friends of the Crespinos and the couple, along with their sons Blake and Kyler, enjoyed being part of the GHS coaching family.

Coach Dave Wutke was a 1976 GHS graduate who had coached with Craig for 15 years. The lifelong Girard resident enjoyed Coach Crespino's enthusiasm and appreciated his ability to make their potentially tedious coaches' meetings something of an event, complete with snacks, beverages, and always a sufficient amount of laughter.

Coach Jeremiah Hudson was a young teacher and only in his second year as a high school football coach. He had not played football beyond his freshman year of high school and had come to Girard with no experience coaching the sport. Coach Crespino had patiently spent hours helping Jeremiah learn the game, and the new coach was grateful for the mentoring.

Coach Nick Cheney was a longtime friend of Craig Crespino. The veteran teacher and coach had been at Baxter Springs High School for many years and had worked closely with Blaise the year Blaise served as their principal. Nick had recently taken an administrative position at a nearby alternative school and given up his coaching duties. His good friend Craig had always hoped he would join his coaching staff, and the 2006 season was going to be their opportunity to finally coach together.

Craig Crespino's death was devastating to each and every one of the Trojan coaches on so many levels. They could not imagine a Girard High School football season without their faithful friend and steadfast leader. Setting aside their own personal grief, the coaches gathered to address the terrible dilemma and discuss the unthinkable. They had to answer the questions no one wanted to ask.

Now what?

Where do we go from here?

Who will coach the Trojans this year?

How does one even go about trying to fill the shoes of a beloved leader under such dreadful circumstances? Not one of the assistant coaches felt called to take on the harrowing assignment. They were ready to support an interim head coach in any way they could, but they were all very certain that they were not prepared to step into the empty—no, *tragically vacated*—shoes left before this grief-stricken team.

Coach Siebert asked Blaise if he would consider taking the charge. Technically, the USD 248 Board of Education prohibited administrators from coaching, knowing that both positions were extremely time-consuming and the quality of work was likely to suffer. Still, having coached with Craig and Blaise for a year, Coach Siebert was aware of the fact that Blaise had the experience and knew the players. Blaise sighed heavily at the thought. Already incredibly busy as building principal, he had to agree with the board. Taking on the responsibilities and duties of the head football coach in addition to his administrative position was simply not practical. The group continued to brainstorm.

In addition to gathering input from the coaching staff, Blaise knew the players' feelings would have to be taken into consideration as well.

"We don't need a new head coach!" several vehemently insisted. The idea of replacing Coach Crespino was unimaginable and downright repugnant to them. "We will play for our assistant coaches this year."

Could they function for a season without a head coach? A symbolic nod to Craig's leadership of his team, even in his absence? It was considered, but as a former head football coach, Blaise knew it was not practical. The assistant coaches concurred. A few of the players came to their principal with suggestions regarding who might be able to step in to lead the

Trojans that season. Blaise listened to their ideas and visited with the prospects.

Over the next few days Blaise made dozens of phone calls. He visited with former coaches, retired coaches, and friends of Coach Crespino. He desperately wanted to find that perfect fit—someone Craig knew and respected, someone who would not drastically change the game plans with which the players were familiar, and, ideally, someone who knew the boys and genuinely wanted the best for them. Those things were exceedingly important to him. For the sake of the players. For the sake of the entire community.

Blaise was aware that the interim coach would be in uncomfortable spotlight. He would have to deal with a barrage of media attention and community scrutiny. That alone was deterrent enough for most, but Blaise continued his search, determined to find the right peg for this terribly unfortunate hole.

The multitude of difficulties made it impossible, however, and ultimately, Blaise found no one who was willing or able to step in and serve in place of the fallen head coach of the Trojans. It was simply too much to ask. He knew that all too well. Blaise spent sleepless nights praying about the situation. He revisited the thoughts and ideas the players had shared with him. He respected their wishes and understood their reasoning, but experience told him their suggestions were simply not feasible.

He had exhausted every possibility on the list of potential coaches. In his heart, he already had the solution. It was not something he wanted to do but rather felt *called* to do.

Finally, Blaise surrendered to the thought that he had not been wanting to entertain.

You have to do this yourself.

St. Mary's Colgan head coach Frank Crespino and son Craig take a minute to discuss strategy during one of Craig's high school football games as quarterback of the Panthers.

Left: Coach Craig Crespino in his element on the sideline during a football game, then celebrating after a victory (right).

Coach Crespino talks to his Girard High School Trojan football players.

Coach Crespino (fifth from right) joins a group of Girard High School students in his yard after they "TPed" the coach's house the night before a game. Coach Crespino loved this tradition!

Blaise and Craig enjoy time together after hours at a school event.

Blaise and Craig announce a GHS basketball game together. The two friends enjoyed any involvement in athletics.

One of the Crespino family's favorite photos of Craig.

The Crespino family in 2005.

Above: The 2006 GHS Trojans made it a habit to pray before every ballgame that fateful season.

Left: Girard High School principal Blaise Bauer steps in as interim head coach of the 2006 Trojan football team after Coach Crespino's tragic death.

In memory of their fallen coach, circular yellow decals with the initials CC were placed on the back of every Girard High School football helmet during the 2006 season.

The Crespino family at the 2021 Annual Craig Crespino Memorial Golf Tournement in Girard. From left, Glenna, Erica's youngest son Dax, being held by Anthony's wife Joanna, Anthony, Erica's husband Zach, and Erica. Erica and Zach's two oldest sons Maddox and Knox are standing in front of the sign.

Back row: Coaches Jeremiah Hudson, Joseph Clark, Craig Siebert, Nick Cheney, Blaise Bauer, Dave Wutke **7th row:** Jace Cobb, Brian Holt, Nathan Geier, Kyle Simons, Cody Pierce, Austin Price, Nolan O'Toole, Brock Burnick **6th row:** Kevin Murphy, Trenton Kichler, Dennis Souza, Jared Twarog, Richard Kraft, David Christmas, Kyle Rentfro, Tyler Edwards, Jeremy Grosstephan **5th row:** Dale Brauer, Kyle Klepac, Dakota Jameson, Dustin Coester, Teague Harris, Ryan Donaldson, Taylor Peak, Josh Creech, Travis Webb **4th row:** Matt DeLange, Cody Cherry, Lonnie Mengarelli, Chris Garrett, Trent Crask, Clancy Goodbody, Chris Goble, Travis Reed, Zach Kimberlin, Adam Spatafora **3rd row:** Kolter DeLange, J.D. Sexton, Chayse Shanholtzer, Joe Gritz, Ben DeLange, Brandon Box, Josh Lorenz, Jonathan Leach, Jacob Smith **2nd row:** Darian Kelly, Kyle Duling, Corey Woods, Andrew Augustin, James Sudduth, Stanley Brown, Ben Paoni, Mike Cook, Phillip Grubb, Jimmy Kirby **Front row:** Drew Cook, Johnny Webb, Brad Vinardi, Tanner Poppe, Taylor Woods, Tyler Bennett, Will Holt, Logan Cherry, Gannon Bauer Not pictured: Trent Geier (Photo courtesy of Girard High School)

Taking the Reins

"Craig was a true ambassador for high school football. He personified everything that was great about the sport and its ability to impact kids."

- Blaise Bauer, Craig's friend and GHS Principal, 2001-2011

Blaise looked ahead to the fall semester. His position as high school principal was an incredibly demanding job. The Bauers' children, now ages 10 to 15, participated in a multitude of sports and school activities, which also kept their family on the go. The thought of assuming another tremendously time-consuming assignment was downright daunting for the busy father of four.

Attempting to juggle the business of managing a high school—and also serving as head football coach—could take a serious toll on him and his family. He considered at length how it would affect his wife Nancy and their children, but they were very supportive. They understood the unimaginable dilemma before him, as well as the unique qualifications that made him the right fit. It simply couldn't be anyone else.

Blaise's next consideration was the team. It had been seven years since Blaise had last coached. The current high school players were in elementary school during his coaching days at Galena and were mere toddlers when he had coached with Craig at Girard. Some of their parents remembered his playing days at Pittsburg State University, but that meant little to the boys. Confident, tall, and imposing, Blaise was a natural leader, but the players only knew him as their high school principal. He was concerned that they would not understand his decision to take on the role of head football coach and feared team morale would suffer if the boys felt like the district had not made a serious effort to find a coach who could help them be successful that year. Winning over their confidence and persuading them to believe in him as a coach would be an obstacle he would have to overcome.

Blaise decided to meet with the senior players. Their support was crucial. They would set the tone for this extremely difficult and unusual season, and the rest of the team would undoubtedly follow their lead. In addition to outlining his plan and getting their support, Blaise wanted the senior players to understand that their response to this tragedy would impact everyone affected by Craig's death. The most beneficial thing they could do for their community was to accept what was, in reality, their *only* realistic option and then move forward with the best possible attitude. It was quite probable that no group of high school seniors had ever had this magnitude of leadership responsibilities thrust upon them.

Blaise called senior captain Trent Crask and asked him to contact the other senior players and invite them to meet with him the next day. The following morning Mr. Bauer stood by his pickup truck in the elementary school parking lot as five somber young men pulled in one by one and joined him. First Trent, then cousins Mike and Drew Cook, and finally Jacob Smith and James Sudduth. A handful of other seniors were unable to make it.

"Hey, fellas. Thanks for meeting with me."

The group was grim and deliberate. The young men trusted their principal to make the best decision he could regarding who would serve as head football coach that year, but they were heartsick at the thought of anyone other than Coach Crespino leading the Trojans.

"I want to visit with you about our head coaching decision," Mr. Bauer began. "I know the team has some strong opinions, and I respect that. It's important that you are comfortable with the person we put in this role. That's a big priority for us."

As the high school principal, Blaise was responsible for the tone of the upcoming school year, and he knew that it would be nearly impossible for an outsider to provide the necessary care and devotion this season would require. The players and the community needed someone they knew and trusted, someone who was familiar with the team and the expectations Coach Crespino had for them.

The boys nodded, although there was no enthusiasm. They didn't want to face the reality of replacing Coach

Crespino, but they realized there was no other choice. The group discussed possible coaches, all of whom Blaise had already vetted, but none of whom felt called to accept the difficult assignment.

No one was comfortable stepping into the formidable situation—including Blaise himself. He had prayed for days that God would show him the person who could take the reins and lead this team—and in fact, the entire community—through this terrible time. He was keenly aware that this football season would have to be a healing force for Girard, and whoever took the charge would carry a heavy load. Although Blaise had accepted that he had been called to do this, the thought of being the torch that rekindled the town's languishing flame was overwhelming. It was imperative that he have the team's support and assistance.

Mr. Bauer presented his solution.

"You know it's really late in the year to find someone to do this. We'd rather not bring in someone new under the circumstances, which just doesn't leave us with a lot of options." He looked for the right words. "Although it's not really what *any* of us want, I think this is something I probably need to do myself."

His expression conveyed the turmoil within him, but he reluctantly made his case.

"We need someone in this position that you know, who can help you heal and give you the opportunity to be successful. I coached with Craig for several years and I understand his football philosophy. And I've been a head coach."

Mr. Bauer shared with the seniors his coaching credentials in order to gain their confidence, but he was more concerned that they understand the impact the decision would have on the entire Girard community. To some degree, he was asking them to think beyond themselves and their teammates and accept what would hopefully be the most healing solution for their town.

"You need someone who will respect your feelings about Coach Crespino and honor his memory throughout the season, but we also need someone who is cognizant of the toll this has taken on our entire student body, our staff, and the community as a whole. So, even though you—*and I*—might have reservations about it, this is the direction we need to go."

The senior delegates weren't completely surprised by their principal's decision. Hints of the proposed arrangement had started to make their way around the small town. They looked at him and nodded their approval. The young men knew Mr. Bauer was their best option. He was a strong and capable leader, had the experience this assignment would require, and they believed that he genuinely wanted to help them salvage their season. They understood that the dire circumstances had left their principal with limited options.

Mr. Bauer was relieved to see their acceptance but looked hard at the boys.

"If I'm going to do this, I have to have your support. I'll be counting on you to help the team move forward. They don't know me as a coach; they only know me as their principal. They'll be looking to you for leadership, and they'll need to know that you believe in me."

The seniors understood the profound task being asked of them and agreed to accept the responsibility.

"You got it. We'll do whatever we have to do to help our team get through this."

The young men shook Mr. Bauer's hand before parting ways. They left the parking lot feeling somewhat better than when they'd arrived. Knowing they would be in the hands of someone they knew and trusted was a tremendous relief. It was one small step in the healing process. A great deal of uncertainty was still ahead, but they believed in their brothers. They trusted that every player on the GHS Trojan football team would do everything they could to honor Coach Crespino's memory that season.

With the acceptance of the senior players, there was one person left for Blaise to consult with—the essential approval he needed before he would step into the position. He picked up the phone and called Glenna. Her wishes were of utmost importance to Blaise, and he very much wanted her input.

"Hi, Glenna," he began somewhat nervously. "I need to discuss something with you, and I want you to be honest. We have to assign a head coach for the season. I want you to know that nobody *wants* to replace Craig. We know that nobody really *can* replace Craig. But someone has to serve as head football coach. I've talked to a lot of people, and no one feels comfortable taking this on. How would you feel if, instead of bringing in someone new, I stepped in and did it for a year?"

The phone call meant a great deal to Glenna. Still reeling with grief, she was grateful for the consideration and not the least bit surprised by the suggestion, as if she'd known all along that there was no other option.

"Blaise," she began, a tremendous sense of peace and graciousness in her voice, "Craig would not have wanted it any other way."

With that, Blaise agreed to serve as head football coach for the 2006 season.

Exactly one week after Craig's death, a special school board meeting was held to approve and announce the decision. Under normal circumstances the board did not allow administrators to coach in any capacity, let alone serve as a *head* coach. But these were not normal circumstances.

"This is a situation that none of us wanted to have to deal with," Superintendent Gary Snawder began. "We need to put somebody in that position who the kids know and trust. Blaise knows this will be difficult, but his willingness to take the reins will help us heal and give us some time to recover."

Aware of the tremendous task ahead of their high school principal, board president Tony Stonerock added, "Everyone is here for you, Blaise."

Board members Ed Becker, Aaron Callaway, Dave Goble, Jim Mengarelli, Gayle Price, and Dale Shireman offered their support as well. They recognized that getting back on the sidelines after being out of coaching for seven years was going to require many hours of preparation, review and study for their high school principal. Tom Stegman, assistant high school principal, would have to shoulder much more of the administrative load this semester, and he readily agreed to take on additional duties.

School patrons and community members offered to watch the Bauer children, promised prayers for the busy family, and brought food to them. It was the community's way of banding together and carrying each other through this difficult time. They had embraced the Crespino family, and they would now embrace the Bauers as well for being willing to be a part of the healing process.

Blaise collected Craig's playbooks and began the arduous process of taking over the head coaching duties and all that entailed. He spent hours poring through Craig's notebooks and watching game films, familiarizing himself with the new system that Craig had recently implemented. Coach Crespino was trying something new offensively; it was a change from what Blaise had run as offensive coordinator years ago when he coached with Craig.

For several nights Blaise studied the new system while the rest of their busy household slept. For the sake of the players, he wanted to change as little as possible. But this new offense was not his own, and as much as he hated the thought of throwing yet another curveball at the team, Blaise was convinced that he needed to dust off his old playbooks and return to what he knew best.

He met with the coaching staff to discuss the idea. Their opinions were critical to Blaise. He would be heavily dependent upon these men this season, especially during this transitional period as he scrambled to get up to speed. There was so much to learn. Blaise wasn't even sure which teams were on the Trojans' 2006 schedule. It was several weeks' worth of preparation, but he didn't have weeks. He had days. The task was positively monumental.

As a group, the Trojan coaches assessed personnel, positions, strategies, and opponents. The assistant coaches concurred that it would be best to return to the veer offense. The players were still familiar with it, so it would not be an enormous change for them. The coaching staff worked long hours making the changes and preparing for the impending season.

Blaise came home exhausted every night. Nancy knelt beside him one evening as he lay on the couch, eyes closed. She stroked his hair and smiled.

"I'm proud of you," she whispered.

Blaise smiled and scoffed modestly.

"This is gonna be a rough few months," he told her.

"We'll get through it," she assured him. "You're the only one who can do this, Blaise. You're still here for a reason. Maybe this is it."

Blaise recalled the decision he'd made just a few short months ago—to stay in Girard, despite the appealing opportunity at the Catholic school. He hugged his wife.

Bloom where you are planted.

The words were little more than a cliche during that fateful phone conversation. Today they were God speaking directly to him, and he was ready to accept the challenge.

CHAPTER 16

Pulling Strings

"Craig and I worked together to use football as a way to keep certain young men in school. Most of them didn't fully realize what he was up to until after they had graduated!"
- Jeff Leslie, Craig's friend and Girard Middle School head football coach, 2005-2014

In the days following the funeral, Glenna, Erica, and Anthony prepared for life without Craig. Glenna readied herself for the upcoming school year, determined to start the year with as much dignity and positivity as possible in Craig's honor. She wanted to help Erica and Anthony understand that they had to move forward, however reluctantly.

The Crespinos had returned to their home in Girard after spending the first few nights with Glenna's brother and family in Frontenac. Despite the many wonderful memories the home held for them, it was difficult to be there without Craig. However, they found solace in being together.

Over the next few weeks, the now family of three spent hours on end writing thank-you notes. More than a thousand cards had to be sent to express gratitude for the outpouring of sympathy they had received. Physically and emotionally exhausted, Erica and Anthony suggested one evening that they put the cards aside and get out of the house for a while.

They decided to go to a casino just a few hours away for a change of scenery and a much-needed break from the reality of their current situation. It was somewhere cool where they could escape the summer heat. A place where they could blend into the crowd and not be in the spotlight. The decision to visit the casino was curious for Glenna, as the family had never been there before. Regardless, it was a welcome reprieve. They were all anxious to change their painful pattern of existence for a bit.

As the family made the two-hour drive, they discussed the upcoming semester. Anthony had received a full music scholarship from nearby Pittsburg State University and would be living at home with Glenna. Erica, however, was preparing for her senior year of college at Wichita State and had another clinical experience awaiting her at a Wichita facility. Under the circumstances, she couldn't bear the thought of being two and a half hours away from family.

"I'm thinking of taking a semester off and staying at home," Erica began.

"It's your senior year, Erica. You can't do that now," Glenna responded sadly. She appreciated her daughter's intentions and wanted nothing more than to have Erica home with her, but she couldn't let her put her life on hold. "Your dad wouldn't want that either."

"I know, but I just feel like we need to be together right now." Erica was struggling with the decision.

The conversation continued without resolution, and eventually, the three arrived at the casino and found a spot near the door. They had no sooner settled in when fellow Girard residents, Dr. Robert Haderlein and his daughter Trisha, walked through the doors of the casino. Both parties were thoroughly surprised to see one another. Dr. Haderlein was a former Girard school board member, and R.V. Haderlein Elementary, where Glenna taught, bore his name because of his significant contributions to education, both locally and nationally. His daughter, Dr. Trisha Self, was one of Erica's supervisors at Wichita State. Dr. Self immediately went to Erica and gave her a warm hug.

"How are you holding up?" the kind woman asked Erica. "You have been on my mind so much!"

"As good as can be expected, I guess," came the somber reply. "I can't believe we ran into each other here!"

"I know. It's such a coincidence! We're on our way back from one of Dad's doctor's appointments in Tulsa and both just needed to get out and stretch our legs," Dr. Self began. "The interesting thing is I've been trying to get ahold of you to tell you that I'm waiving the requirement that your upcoming clinical be in the Wichita area. We've reached out to a facility in Pittsburg, and they have agreed to accommodate a clinical experience for you so that you can be closer to family."

The Crespinos were absolutely elated. They hugged them both, thanked Dr. Self, and agreed to be in contact to work out the details. It was the best thing that had happened to them in the days since Craig's death, and it felt like someone was pulling some strings for them.

Glenna smiled a knowing smile and said to herself, *Thank you, Craig.*

The Crespino family left the casino that evening feeling lighter. This new arrangement was an answer to prayers they had not yet even uttered, and they all felt Craig's warm, welcome presence in the odd coincidence of running into Erica's supervisor in such an unusual place.

The upcoming school year now seemed less daunting to all three of them. They would be together, and in light of their painful circumstances, that was by far the best place to be. The comfort and strength they found in each other was as essential as air. A future without their beloved husband and father seemed insurmountable, but they were determined to honor Craig by pressing on—together. They simply had no other choice.

CHAPTER 17

Football Camp Begins

"The night after my brother was killed (in a car accident), Coach Crespino sat on my couch writing Geramie's eulogy. This man made every effort to come to me and help me through my brother's death. He was always there whenever I needed him and he became a father to me."
- Nicholas Kirby, GHS Class of 2007

Gold rubber wristbands with the word "COACH" embossed into them were quickly becoming a staple around Girard, a bright visual reminder that this season was dedicated to Coach Crespino. Players and coaches, students and staff members, parents and fans—even Trojan opponents—were well aware of the deep, emotional overtones this season would have for the Girard community.

No one seemed more aware of the enormity of the situation than the local media, however. Coach Crespino's death had a devastating and reverberating effect on the entire area. News crews recognized the fact that this story was not going away. People were captivated by it because it was so unbelievable. So inconceivable. Even ESPN caught wind of the terrible tragedy and reported it nationally. Girard players and coaches were receiving a multitude of phone calls, and reporters were calling the school and the board office as well. The story was taking on a life of its own.

"This is a problem," Blaise told Superintendent Gary Snawder. He was exasperated at the amount of time he was spending on the phone and could see that it had the potential to become a serious distraction for the players. "Can you shut this down? At least until our first game? We need to be able to have camp and conduct practices without the constant disruption of cameras and reporters. Our players need to be able to focus on the game. They need time to heal, and they have to be allowed to move on from Craig's death."

Mr. Snawder called all of the local television stations, newspapers, and radio stations and requested that they respect the privacy of the players and coaches, the Crespino family, and the Girard community in general as they tried to heal and move forward. He conceded that once the season started, reporters would be allowed to attend practices and interview players and coaches, but until the week of the first game, the media was essentially banished.

The Trojan football camp was rescheduled to start on Monday, July 31, one week after the original start date and ten days after Coach Crespino's death. This required special permission from the Kansas High School Athletics Association, as the original camp date was actually the latest allowed.

Because of the extraordinary circumstances, permission was granted.

The Trojans would meet for football camp on the very field where their beloved coach had lost his life. The decision to do so was not an easy one, and more than a few eyebrows were raised when it was made public, but Blaise knew they would have to return to the field eventually. He was convinced it was best to deal with the emotional trauma head-on, rather than avoiding or postponing it.

For some of the players the practice field had been a peaceful nighttime hangout over the years. Removed from the lights and modest bustle of town, the field provided a quiet retreat for the teens, who would lay on the hoods of their cars staring up at the stars, talking for hours or listening to music late into the night.

But after the terrible accident, they wondered if they could ever see it as the welcoming space it had once been. Tyler Edwards and Ben Paoni, along with their friend Shane Duling, decided to make a visit to the field one night during the week their football camp was supposed to have taken place.

They parked their cars at the edge of the field and stepped out into the darkness, suddenly unsure if they were ready to be there. The sky was clear and the stars were bright. Fireflies twinkled haphazardly above the dark expanse. A hushed breeze made its way through the leaves of surrounding trees, offering up a silky whisper. The lulling song of crickets in the tall surrounding grasses and the distant trill of frogs in area ponds quieted their heavy heartbeats.

The contradiction of the tranquil scene and the horrific

tragedy that had taken place there just days earlier struck the young men. They lay on the hoods of their cars and let their grief drift up to the heavens, each of them imagining what advice and consolation Coach would have had for them at a time such as this.

The coaching staff arrived at the practice field early that Monday morning. Blaise came prepared to focus on football. He had made a conscious decision that he was not going to dwell on the tragic loss of their head coach—or use it as motivation. That was completely unnecessary. He was painfully aware of how Craig's death had affected the players. The best thing he could do for them was to help them move forward. He knew it was important for them to be together and that focusing on football would help them shake the fog of grief that enveloped them—even if just for a few hours a day.

Jace pulled up to the field that sunny summer morning. He sat in his car and mentally prepared himself to step onto that field again. It was the first time he'd been there since the accident. As an experienced student trainer who had worked closely with Craig, Jace would be invaluable to Blaise. He and fellow trainer Brian Holt were given an unprecedented amount of responsibility that season, and Blaise was incredibly grateful for their help. The two teens were always ready and willing to assist with the little details the interim coach simply didn't have time for.

Being on the practice field was different though. The memories of the accident came flooding back to Jace. It was still very difficult to accept the idea that Coach would not be a part of this football season, would not be a part of any football season, not ever again. Jace was not sure he was ready to tackle the emotions that were churning inside him, but he slowly opened his car door anyway and stepped out.

One by one, the players began to arrive as well. Most of them had not been to the field since the accident, and their attention was immediately drawn to the west end of the north field. At the spot where the accident had occurred was a patch of worked-up soil—reseeded and covered in straw—which practically screamed at them. It was a callous reminder of the emotional burden they would have to carry this football season.

The players were sullen and unsure. This was their first football-related activity without Coach Crespino. The finality of his absence became real, and it was agonizing. The man they could have turned to with their pain—the man who would have helped them work through it—was no longer there. The mood was as heavy as the thick Kansas summer air. Oppressive. Blaise anticipated this. Before any talk of football began, he gathered the team in a circle and led the group in prayer.

"Lord, we ask for your help today. Help us get through this morning. Help us get through this season. Help us to be a comfort to each other, to our families, and to our community during this difficult time. We know that this football season is about more than football. This football season we have much bigger goals than other teams. Our number one goal is to overcome the adversity that has been dealt to these young men. I know that this is not going to be our best camp, Father, so help us to be patient. Help us to simply do our best today—and every day this season. Help us to dedicate our efforts to

Coach Crespino for all that he was to this football team and this community."

Together, the team said the Lord's Prayer and finished with "Amen." With that, the 2006 Girard High School Trojan Summer Football Camp finally began.

It was awkward and terrible at first. Players and coaches alike wore an uncomfortable cloak of guilt and sadness. Pressing on, the coaches began with the fundamentals. Lining up, blocking, running through a few plays. Players were distracted and anxious. There was nothing to do but push forward and try to convince themselves that everything was going to be okay.

Offensive drills began, and Tyler Bennett was taking snaps at quarterback. Tyler's father, Mike Bennett, and his uncle, Bryan Mahnken, had been Blaise's teammates in college, so Tyler had already received an earful about his principal's former football prowess. Still, for the cocky high school quarterback, the men's college days were ancient history. He respected Mr. Bauer as his high school principal, but this new title of "Coach" would have to be earned.

Tyler's emotions were still raw. He struggled to focus on the drills and not on his grief; he knew the team needed a strong leader this year. The weight of the responsibility was heavy on his mind, but he was determined to make the best of the season for the sake of his teammates.

Midway through the morning, as Mr. Bauer was demonstrating a technique to the offensive squad, a flutter of white drew Tyler's attention from the coach. It was a white bird, now sitting in a nearby tree. Tyler began to walk toward the bird, fixated on the meaning of this rather unusual visitor.

"Tyler?" Mr. Bauer called out to his quarterback, unsure what was luring the young man away.

Tyler looked back as if to say, *Do you see this, too?*

"Come back to the huddle," Mr. Bauer motioned, sympathetic but also determined not to allow emotional diversions to disrupt the team's journey forward.

Tyler walked back to the team, still somewhat distracted by the haunting image. He was not the only one who noticed the bird. Craig's nephew and assistant coach, Joseph Clark, saw it, too. It was likely a dove, not unheard of in this part of the Midwest, but most Kansas doves are a soft brown. This particular bird was pure white, and it seemed almost as interested in the players as they were in it. The spiritual symbolism was not lost on anyone who saw it. They all wanted desperately to believe that Coach was there with them in some capacity. The bird's presence was curious, but also reassuring and comforting.

Later in the morning, a misdirected pass soared over a receiver's head and rolled into the hallowed straw patch. Everyone froze as several uncomfortable seconds passed. The players looked at each other pensively. Finally, a freshman player ran in, grabbed it, and tossed it back into play. Drills continued, and no one brought it up again.

Around noon, the coaches gathered the team in a circle to conclude the first morning of the five-day camp. They had made it through one day without being swallowed up by the grief that had threatened to consume them the minute they walked onto that field. This simple achievement was another small step forward, and it felt like a victory.

The first couple days of camp were somber and difficult,

to be sure. The players tried their best to focus on the game, and not on the terrible tragedy that had taken place on their field of play. But always, always that patch of straw beckoned, disrupting their thoughts and rattling their nerves.

Eventually, however, the patch became a shrine of sorts. Players would arrive early for camp and spend time kneeling beside it. Many stayed afterward to do the same. Remembering Coach Crespino. Conversing with him. Praying. It made them feel closer to him and helped them come to terms with what he would have wanted from them—and *for* them.

The white bird became a constant. The players and coaches came to view it as a symbol that their beloved Coach was watching over them in his own way. Each day of camp became just a little easier, a little less painful and awkward, a little more focused. The pure joy of the game began to creep into the drills, and a new sentiment prevailed: *Determination*.

The team's sweat and effort, their revelry and camaraderie were not an affront to their deceased coach. For 22 years Coach Crespino brought young men to this field for those exact purposes. He would have wanted nothing less for this group of players. Day after day, as this sank in, the players worked harder and harder. They found solace in each other and in their coaches. A brotherhood was forming because of their mutual loss, and a conviction to carry each other drove them. They were going to survive this common tragedy as a team, by focusing on the game that meant so much to Coach Crespino and giving everything they had. They would leave it all on the field and be the best they could be. They would win.

And they would do it for Coach.

CHAPTER 18

The First Game

"Craig impacted the lives of so many. He was a great man, a great coach, and a great friend. He will forever be remembered and missed."
- Craig Siebert, GHS Class of 1989; GHS football coach, 1993-2018

Because their summer football camp had been postponed a week, the Trojans started conditioning the week immediately after camp, and then regular team practices the following week. The lack of downtime was just fine with the players and their coaches. It kept them together and gave them something positive to focus on. Craig's death had received unprecedented media attention over the last few weeks, and the team was ready to focus on the game, not the terrible tragedy that had unfortunately become synonymous with Girard football.

The Trojan coaching staff had returned to the veer offense. It was a good fit for their current roster. Other than the fact that they were no longer in the shotgun formation, it was not a significant change for the players. Junior Tyler Bennett would be the starting quarterback. Intelligent and athletic, Tyler was well equipped for the role.

With the option offense and veer formation, running back assignments were critical. Senior Mike Cook would shoulder the majority of the duties in the backfield. Sturdy and strong, Mike worked hard for every inch and was an intimidating force for opposing defenses to try to contain. Coaches were excited about sophomore Darian Kelly as well. A gifted athlete who excelled on the basketball court, Darian was probably better suited for the football field, and his coaches were anxious to find out. Senior Trent Geier, junior Philip Grubb, and sophomores Taylor Woods and Stanley Brown would also carry the ball at times.

Viable threats at wide receiver and tight end rounded out the Trojan option attack. Returning senior wide receiver Drew Cook was expected to have another exciting season, while juniors Corey Woods and Joe Grilz would provide additional deep threats. Junior Ben Paoni and sophomore Tanner Poppe would see time at tight end. Trojan coaches would count on them to spread out the defense to account for the pass. This would open up the middle for Bennett and the backs but also give the Trojans a dependable pass option.

The Trojan offensive line was experienced and solid, with seniors Jacob Smith, Trent Crask, Ryan Donaldson and Dustin Coester lending leadership. Brawny junior lettermen Lonnie Mengarelli, Matt DeLange, and Tyler Edwards returned to offer their assistance as well.

Crask, Mengarelli, Edwards, Coester and Donaldson

would also play on the defensive side of the line, wreaking havoc alongside Mike Cook, Josh Creech, Dennis Souza, and Dakota Jameson. At inside linebacker, Joe Grilz, Jacob Smith, and Philip Grubb would bridle opponents while Trent Geier, Brad Vinardi, Ben DeLange, Tanner Poppe, and Taylor Woods would split time at outside linebacker.

The ten senior players set a strong, positive tone for the team. Dustin Coester was dependable on and off the field; his teammates knew they could count on him. Drew Cook was a smooth, talented athlete with the ability to gracefully snatch a pass out of the air or block a defender into the ground. Mike Cook brought an energy to the team; his strength and agility were game changers on both sides of the ball. Trent Crask was a tremendous asset for the coaches. Smart and reliable, Trent knew every player's assignment and was like another coach on the field. Ryan Donaldson and Trent Geier were two of the hardest workers on the team. Their work ethic and willingness to do whatever was asked of them set a solid example for underclassmen. Jacob Smith was strong and dependable with an ability to make big hits and big plays. Brad Vinardi was a tough, gritty player with a knack for being in the right place at the right time. James Sudduth, although injured and unable to play that season, provided critical positivity and was always the first to encourage his teammates. As a group, these ten players led by example, and the Trojan coaches were grateful for their leadership.

Practice felt different from other years. Things were lighter. Frustrations and tempers that might have flared in previous years were simply not an issue. Players were using practice to have fun and to forget about their heartache and loss. They were a band of brothers dedicated to getting through this season together. They would take care of each other, lift each other up. They would never tear each other down. Not this year. There just wasn't any room for it.

School started in mid-August, and once again emotions ran high. Students felt every "first" like a kick in the gut. The first time they saw Coach Crespino's empty parking space. The first time they walked past his office. The first time they went to social studies or weights class, and he wasn't there. It was like ripping the scab off a wound. Coach Crespino loved "his kids," and his absence pained them deeply.

The school mood was somber. And yet, there was a peaceful camaraderie among the students, as if they knew how much their peers and teachers were hurting. Normally rowdy, rebellious students were downright helpful and polite. Cliques softened, even if just temporarily, and students who did not typically intermingle were seen consoling one another. There was an unspoken understanding that this is what Coach would have wanted. It was a lovely tribute to a man who cared about everyone.

The first game on the Trojans' schedule was set for 7 p.m. on Friday, September 1, against the Riverton Rams. It was a home game, thankfully. The coaches knew the players would be anxious and feeling the pressure. They didn't need the added strain of traveling to an opponent's home turf.

Blaise tried to prepare for the fact that the media would be back in full force once they were given the green light. He was not looking forward to that. Calls started coming in early that week, and he spent more time than he would have liked on the phone with reporters. There was a constant media presence at practices. Players were interviewed and asked how Coach Crespino's death had impacted the team, a rather inane question but not unexpected.

Inside the school, GHS cheerleaders covered the high school halls with banners and signs, many of them indicating that this game, this season, was for Coach Crespino. Game programs were printed with a full-page dedication to the fallen coach. The tribute featured a large, color photo of Craig in a white coaching shirt with a whistle around his neck. Under it were the words: "In loving memory of Coach Craig Crespino, Sept. 23, 1960 to July 21, 2006." It was decided that a head coach would not be designated in the program. Instead, all of the coaches' names were listed under one heading: Coaches.

The beginning of the football season was difficult for the Crespino family. They remembered the excitement in their house as the first Trojan football game approached each year. Their lives revolved around Girard football. They lived and breathed it. But this year was so tragically different. The family discussed whether they would go to the first game, whether they could handle it emotionally. Craig's death was so recent and the grief still so very raw.

One evening that week, Glenna's uncle, Dennis Franchione, called to check on them. Franchione had been the head football coach at Pittsburg State University during Blaise's tenure as a college football player but was now head football coach at Texas A&M University. Glenna told him of their dilemma, and her uncle offered the family another option. He invited them to fly down to College Station to watch his Aggies play instead. It was Labor Day weekend and also Glenna's birthday, and the Crespino family decided to accept the invitation. The three would drive to Tulsa Friday night and then fly out for Texas Saturday morning. It was something to look forward to, a welcome escape from the painful reality that was their life in Girard at the moment.

That Friday night was warm and calm, but the atmosphere was alive. The Trojans' matchup against the Riverton Rams was the most highly anticipated high school game in the area. After losing their head coach just three days before their summer camp, the Girard Trojans were the human-interest story of the year. Everyone wanted to be a part of this season, to cheer on this team for whom all of southeast Kansas mourned. The tragic start of their season left everyone wishing them a positive and successful year, but no one was quite sure how these young men would respond to the loss. Expectations were intense.

The cheerleaders formed a tunnel at the edge of the east end zone, and the Girard Trojans stampeded out of the locker room, through the tunnel, and onto the football field for their season-opening game. They were wearing the brand-new uniforms that Coach Crespino had chosen for them the previous spring. Watching through the fence from outside the stadium was Glenna. The family's bags were packed, and they would be leaving soon for Tulsa, but she simply couldn't miss the boys running out in their new uniforms for the first time. She knew how proud Craig would have been and had to be there for it. However, the heartache of seeing the Girard Trojans run onto the field without Craig for the first time in 22 years was more than she could bear. She quietly and tearfully slipped back into her car and left for home.

In the stands the crowd rose to their feet in support of this squad of young men whose football season had been decidedly difficult before it even began. Seniors Trent Crask and Jacob Smith clasped hands and walked to the center of the field for the coin toss. The visiting team captains called "heads" as the quarter flickered upward and down again. It landed on the grass, heads up. The Rams chose to receive, and the team captains exchanged handshakes and extended traditional "good luck" sentiments before hustling back to their respective sidelines.

The Trojan kickoff team and the Ram return team took the field and got into position. Team quarterback and kicker Tyler Bennett stood behind the line of scrimmage with his arm in the air, ready to signal his team into action. The crowd yelled and waved, wild with anticipation. With a swing of the referee's arm and the sound of his whistle, the first game of the 2006 Girard Trojan football season began.

Tyler sent a solid kick deep into Ram territory. After a short kickoff return, the special teams bustled off the field as Riverton's offense headed out for their first series of the season. Three running plays in a row resulted in a gain of very little against the tough Trojan defense. Facing fourth down with several yards to go, they punted the ball to the Trojans.

It was time for Girard's offensive debut. Tyler took the snap from center Matt DeLange and quickly handed the ball to Phillip Grubb. Phillip darted through the Riverton defense, gaining 34 yards and a first down for the Trojans, just inside Ram territory. The offensive line got set, and Tyler took his second snap of the night. He stepped back and tossed the ball to Darian Kelly, who ran it another 13 yards to the Ram 33-yard line. On the third play of the series, Tyler kept the ball himself and sped through Riverton defenders all the way into the end zone for a touchdown. The Girard Trojans were off to a promising start.

A bobbled snap on the PAT (point after touchdown) derailed the kick and cost them the extra point, but they had put the first points on the board, which felt good. Trojans led 6-0.

Girard's defense forced Riverton to go three-and-out on their next series as well. They punted the ball but regained possession after a Trojan fumble. A costly penalty kept the Rams from breaching the goal line, but they were able to put three points on the board with a successful field goal, and the Trojans' lead was cut to 6-3.

Girard ran the subsequent kickoff back to their own 35-yard line. Despite several penalties and dropped passes, the Trojans steadily moved the ball to within 10 yards of the Ram end zone. Costly miscues continued to plague the series, however, and they were forced to bring out their field goal unit. Girard settled for three points, increasing their lead to 9-3.

It was a sloppy first half for both teams, marred by penalties, turnovers, and poor execution. With just a minute left in the half, the Trojans once again had possession of the ball and were hoping to pad their small lead before halftime. They were not playing up to their potential, and they knew it.

The Trojans started their final series of the half on their own 36-yard line. Tyler dropped back and aired it out on first down. In a flash of blue, a Riverton defender picked off the pass and was in the Trojan end zone before their offense even knew what had happened. Tyler hung his head, angry with himself for the turnover. He jogged off the field and watched from the sideline as the Ram kicker sent the ball through the uprights for the extra point. Rams led 10-9, with just seconds left in the first half.

A sense of nervousness itched through the crowd. Unsure of what to expect from these shell-shocked boys, no one seemed too surprised at the Trojans' less-than-stellar performance so far.

The game clock gave up its last ticks of the half, and the players hustled off the field and into the locker room. Coach Bauer was not pleased with the team's performance. He had high expectations for them and felt like they had played poorly for the majority of the half, but he also realized that they were just plum rattled. It had been a long week. Hounded by reporters and pressured by community expectations, the team was feeling the strain and it was taking a toll.

"Well, we got that out of our system," he said with a feigned smile. Coach Bauer took a deep breath before continuing.

"I know this has been a traumatic few weeks. The press has been a distraction. Emotions are high. You've been through a lot. There are a lot of expectations on you this season, and most of them have nothing to do with football."

He looked hard at the faces before him. He saw frustration, stress, disappointment. They were buckling under the weight of the constant publicity and media attention, the emotional whirlwind that engulfed them, the uncertainty of a season without their trusted leader, and the fear of disappointing everyone who loved Coach Crespino. The pressure on these teenage boys was palpable. Brutal. Unfair.

Coach Bauer paused, looking for the right words.

"Look, you're better than this team. You are. You're just putting too much pressure on yourselves. Just go out there and play football."

"Execute."

"Do your job."

"Have fun."

The players left the locker room after halftime, and the team captains gathered the squad outside the building.

"Coach Bauer's right. We're better than this! Is this how we show what Coach meant to us? Is this all we've got for him? Let's go make him proud!"

With a renewed sense of determination and confidence, they sprinted back onto the field, fired up and ready to play. The second half was a completely different ballgame. The Trojans were sharp and focused. They scored 20 unanswered points in the third quarter and another seven in the fourth, securing their first victory with a 36-10 win over the Riverton Rams.

The Girard coaches met briefly after the game. They were not surprised by the way their team had played. They knew they could execute, if they could stay focused, but they feared this season would be racked by distractions, inconsistency, and emotional turmoil.

Coach Bauer headed home with the evening's game film and spent a few hours analyzing the Trojans' performance as Friday night slipped into the wee hours of Saturday morning.

Before they could prepare for next week's opponent, they would have to address their own mistakes. As both principal and head football coach, Blaise did not have time to waste getting started.

An exhausted sigh slipped through his lips as he finally lay down to sleep late that night. One game down. They had survived the first week of the season. Blaise was hopeful that the worst was behind them, but he feared it most likely was not.

CHAPTER 19

Finding Their Rhythm

"Coach Crespino treated every player as if they were his son. Always there to pick you up, pat you on the back, and keep you moving forward."
- Trent Crask, GHS Class of 2007

The victory over Riverton seemed to ease the pressure on the team a bit. The players' moods lifted, and they were energized. The Trojan coaches, however, were concerned with the number of errors they had seen in their first game, and were determined to work out the kinks and make sure the Trojans were playing up to their potential.

"Do it again!" Coach Bauer barked at the offense that Monday afternoon at practice.

Tyler and the offense ran the play again, but it was still not what their coach wanted of them. Coach Bauer cued Tyler to run the play once more. He stepped onto the field with his clipboard still in his hand and ran the tight end route himself to show the boys how to do it—making a perfect one-handed catch. Tyler smiled, impressed. Mr. Bauer had earned his respect and trust in the few weeks since he had taken the reins. He had also earned the title "Coach."

The brotherhood of the Trojan football team was not exclusive to the players; the coaches were family, too. These six men had set out to do whatever was necessary to help the players overcome a horrific start to their high school football season, and the team genuinely loved and appreciated them for that.

In addition to after-school practices, high school football coaches meet first thing every Saturday morning to analyze game film, each coach having a different aspect of the game to break down and record. The final report gives them an overview of their opponent's tendencies, strong and weak sides, and various formations. From there they create their game plan for the upcoming week. The process takes several hours, but dedicated coaches understand that it is necessary to succeed. In preparation for the more critical games and certainly during the postseason, they will often spend their Sundays at the school as well. There are no weekends for a football coach during football season. That just comes with the territory.

The Trojans practiced hard for their upcoming game against the Northeast Vikings that week. Just nine miles east of Girard, Northeast High School in Arma, Kansas, was a considerably smaller school than Girard and had struggled to find success on the football field. The Trojan coaches would not overlook any opponent, however, and took every game seriously. The players echoed their intensity. It was their way of honoring Coach Crespino, and they were dogged in their pursuit of a season that would make him proud.

On Friday, September 8, the Northeast Vikings loaded their bus and made the short drive to Frank Jameson Field on the Girard High School campus. With only 23 players on their roster, they had fewer than half the number of players on the Trojan sideline and were the smallest team numbers-wise that Girard would face this season.

Trojan fans were excited about the team's first victory, and the anticipation in the stands was unmistakable. Glenna, Erica, and Anthony were in attendance this week after their much-needed getaway last weekend. The school district had arranged a pregame presentation to honor Craig. The Crespinos, including Craig's parents, Frank and JoAnn, were invited onto the field. A moment of silence was offered in memory of Coach Crespino, and the family was given a football with Craig's likeness on it.

The gesture was a genuine outpouring of love and support for the family, but the attention was unnerving for Glenna. She was used to Craig being in the spotlight. He was the outgoing one, the one who thrived in the limelight. Glenna clung tightly to her children as she felt the swarm of eyes focused on her. She desperately wished to be in the stands instead, preparing to watch her husband and his beloved Trojans storm the field. This new reality was utterly uncomfortable.

The Crespinos made their way back to their seats in the stadium as the high school band took the field for the national anthem. Nancy Bauer had invited Glenna and family to sit with her and had held seats for them. The two women had formed a special bond. Nancy had arranged weekly dinners with Glenna and Erica since Craig's death. They would eat at the Bauer home and then watch a movie. Occasionally, Nancy and her daughters would bring the meal to the Crespino home, along with a rented movie. It was most appreciated by Glenna, as everyday tasks as simple as cooking often got lost in the grief that consumed the family.

Glenna settled into her seat and looked on as the band played . . . the cheerleaders formed their tunnel . . . the players ran onto the field . . . the crowd cheered. It was the same Friday night scene she'd lived a hundred times. And yet it was not the same. It would never be the same again. Life was going on around her, but for Glenna, time had stopped. It was surreal and painful, but she was there. She was present. She wanted to continue to do the things that Craig loved, the things they had done together. However, without Craig, there was no longer joy in them.

Seeing her nephew Joseph on the field as a coach was very special though. He had been so excited when Craig hired him to be a part of the 2006 coaching staff. The fact that he was out there kept a little bit of Craig on the field for Glenna and brought her some measure of comfort. She smiled as she realized that this was the fulfillment of a dream for Joseph, regardless of the terrible circumstances.

Having Blaise on the field with the team was also comforting for Glenna. She knew that he would have been Craig's choice to step in that year. The two men respected each other tremendously, and she appreciated Blaise's willingness to help "Craig's kids" through this incredibly difficult time.

Following the coin toss, the teams took the field. The

Trojans kicked off to the Vikings, who attempted a handful of rushing plays, but the Trojan defense stifled all efforts. Northeast was forced to punt, and Girard ran the kick back to their own 45-yard line. With the help of a 35-yard pass from Tyler Bennett to Drew Cook, the Trojans marched down the field. Just three and a half minutes into the game, they were able to run the ball in for a touchdown on their first series.

And so went the rest of the game. The Vikings struggled to move the ball as the Trojan defense disrupted every maneuver, while Girard's offense was able to move the ball almost at will. They accrued an impressive 435 yards of offense, scoring six touchdowns and a field goal. The Trojans advanced to 2-0 with a 43-0 win over the Northeast Vikings.

The victory over Northeast was a good one, but the Girard coaches were still concerned with the number of penalties the Trojans were drawing. Setting themselves back 85 yards, they had been flagged 11 times over the course of the ballgame. They would have to be better prepared mentally if they hoped to defeat next week's opponent, the undefeated Frontenac Raiders.

The Raiders had finished second in the state the previous year. They were always a physical opponent and seemed to be on every school's rivalry list. To make matters worse, it would be Girard's first away game, and Frontenac was a tough place to play. Their small stands were always packed full of loud fans who made it their mission to impact the game in every way possible.

Preparations for next Friday's game began immediately after Blaise returned home that night. Once again, as his family slept, the dedicated coach watched the evening's game film in his living room and took notes. He saw some good things happening, but he also saw a frustrating number of mental errors and miscues.

The Girard coaches met Saturday morning to break down film and create their game plan for the upcoming week. They were determined to make sure mistakes and penalties were addressed and eliminated. The Trojans would have to bring their A-game if they hoped to beat the undefeated Raiders.

Practice went well that week. The team looked sharp and things were clicking. The Trojans felt good. They were on a roll and their confidence was high. Frontenac's home-field advantage would not deter them. They had made a commitment to play like champions in honor of their beloved Coach, and they were prepared to take care of business.

The sun was still shining brightly that Friday afternoon as the Trojans' bus pulled onto the Frontenac High School campus. Summer was reluctant to give up its hold on the Midwest, and the temperature was high for mid-September. The team unloaded and began their pregame routine, serious and intent.

Former Frontenac Raider Joseph Clark, who had once been so excited to coach the Trojans with his uncle, looked on as the team readied themselves for the night's contest. He could sense the impact Craig had made on these young men. They understood his expectations for them, even though he wasn't there to affirm them. Their determination to honor Coach Crespino's hopes and goals for them was heartwarming for him.

The pregame clock ticked down to zero, and the special teams assembled on their respective ends of the field. Along the perimeter fence, Glenna, Erica, and Anthony stood with Glenna's brother Joe and Craig's father Frank. They knew the Trojans would be playing hard for Coach and were determined to be there to support them.

The first half proved disappointing for both camps. The teams were each able to move the ball for long drives, but inevitably, a costly error would subvert their progress. Going into the game, Girard and Frontenac coaches alike feared that mental mistakes could cost them a win. Frustration was looming large on both sidelines.

The game remained scoreless until late in the first quarter when Trojan running back Darian Kelly broke loose for a 53-yard touchdown run. Tyler's PAT kick added another point to the score, and the Trojans took a 7-0 lead. It was the only scoring drive of the first half for either team.

When the second quarter gave way to halftime, the two teams headed into the locker rooms. Once again, adjustments were made and encouragement was given. Blaise had settled into the role of head coach as one returns to a favorite chair. It was welcoming and comfortable. He had missed the game and the relationships with the players and coaches.

The veteran coach was impressed with this group of young men and pleased with the progress they were making. There was a lot of talent on this Trojan team, and he wondered how opposing coaches could have picked them to finish fourth in the league. It was the lowest he could remember the Trojans ever being picked. He felt sure that they could finish higher than that, but there was an emotional ball and chain attached to this team, the effects of which remained to be seen. A win over Frontenac would go a long way in boosting their confidence.

What the first and second quarters lacked in excitement, the third quarter made up for. The Girard Trojans came out swinging. On the opening play of the half, Darian returned the kickoff all the way to the Raider 35-yard line. The ball was put in his hands again on the very next play, and this time he breached the goal line, adding six points to the Trojans' score. A failed PAT left the lead at 13-0.

Girard's defense played outstanding as well, handing Frontenac another futile series and forcing them to punt. An impressive return set the Trojans up for a 25-yard touchdown run by Tyler Bennett, and a successful two-point conversion gave them a 21-0 lead. Darian returned a punt 80 yards for yet another touchdown before the Raiders scored their first points of the night.

By the time the final seconds of the game ticked away, Darian had scored four touchdowns and a two-point conversion. A final score of 34-14 put Girard's record at 3-0. The Trojans had found their rhythm, and their gifted running back was the talk of the CNC League. Although his first love was basketball, Darian was proving to be a formidable force on the football field. The talented sophomore's speed and agility were difficult for opponents to defend.

But the Trojan's next matchup wasn't against just any opponent. Besides being Craig Crespino's alma mater, Colgan's football program boasted a winning streak of 63 consecutive regular-season games and four state championships. It had been seven years since Girard had defeated Colgan in football, and the Trojans had been outscored 39-215 during that span. The Colgan Panthers football program was nothing short of a dynasty. Current coach Chuck Smith had succeeded Frank Crespino as head coach of the Panthers, and he was also Craig's close friend. In fact, many of the Colgan faithful loved Craig as much as the Girard community and were deeply emotional at the thought of playing Girard and not seeing Craig Crespino on the opposing sideline. The game atmosphere would be heavy—with intense rivalry, unprecedented publicity, and unimaginable grief.

CHAPTER 20

Facing the Dynasty

"He always asked about our family - always! So considerate of others, even if we were competitors. A true Christian soul."
- Susie Lundy, Craig's friend and St. Mary's Colgan patron

The Trojan coaching staff stood on the south sideline of Hutchinson Field that Friday, September 22, and watched as their team ran pregame warmups. The players came determined to take down the Colgan dynasty in honor of Coach Crespino and tension was high.

"They're too amped up," Coach Bauer said, shaking his head. "This isn't good."

An avid student of the game, Blaise was aware that too much adrenaline would cause mental errors and physical fatigue. The coaches looked at each other nervously.

The significance of this game could not be overstated.

Craig loved his alma mater, but once the game clock started, he wanted nothing more than to beat them, and the players knew this. They desperately wanted to defeat Colgan for Coach Crespino, but perhaps the pressure they had put on themselves was simply too much. There was only one way to find out.

The coaches called the team to the sideline, clearing the field for the marching band. The boys rocked and twitched as the national anthem played. They'd have to settle down or it was going to be a long night.

The game began with a short drive by the Panthers. The Trojan defense put pressure on their quarterback, creating confusion. After only a handful of plays, Colgan was forced to punt the ball. The Trojan offense didn't fare much better, however, and was soon preparing to punt as well. Team punter and quarterback Tyler Bennett was deep in the backfield awaiting the snap. On his cue the center thrust the ball toward him. The high snap sailed over his head, and Tyler scrambled after it, hoping to save the play. He managed to retrieve the ball and complete a pass, but his receiver was brought down short of the first-down marker and the Panthers took over on the Trojan 30-yard line.

With only 30 yards between them and the first points of the game, the Colgan Panthers needed just two plays to put the ball in the end zone. A successful PAT kick followed, and Colgan took a 7-0 lead.

Mere seconds after leaving the field, the Trojan offense was putting on their helmets and heading back out. They put together an impressive drive, moving the ball 73 yards down the field before Tyler carried the ball into the Colgan end zone.

He tacked on another point with a line drive PAT, tying the game, 7-7.

The offensive squad lumbered off the field, breathless and depleted. The Trojan coaches watched their weary warriors struggling to recover. Too much adrenaline. They were hopeful that the Panthers would take some time with their next drive, giving the boys a critical opportunity to rest. But their opponents were unable to gain much ground and with fourth and long looming promptly brought out their punt team.

The Trojan offense returned to the field for their third series of the game. On first down Tyler kept the ball and ran. The Panther defense brought him down at the Trojan 40-yard line. As he hit the ground, the ball popped loose and was quickly buried in blue jerseys. It was ruled a fumble, and Colgan was given the ball. Now just 40 yards from their next score, Colgan persistently pushed the ball down the field and into the end zone. The PAT kick gave them a 14-7 lead.

The Trojans would answer on their next series, driving 70 yards to the 2-yard line. Powerful senior running back Mike Cook took the handoff and carried a host of defenders with him into the end zone. It was a crowd-pleasing effort, and Girard fans went berserk!

The PAT team set up, and the ball was snapped. Tyler sent it toward the uprights, but it was blocked. No good. The Trojans would have to settle for six. They trailed 14-13 with just minutes left in the half.

The kickoff team lined up, ready to deliver the ball to the Panthers. If their defense could stay strong for a few more minutes, Girard could go into the locker room at halftime with only a one-point deficit. Coach Bauer figured that would be an acceptable margin, all things considered. He was anxious for the mid-game break which would allow the Trojans to recuperate.

Tyler sent the ball soaring downfield. It was caught at the Colgan 25-yard line, and the Panther returner took off for the Trojan end of the field. He skirted around tackles and passed the 35, slipped through the hands of defenders and crossed the 45 before finally being caught at midfield. Coach Bauer shook his head. Another short distance for Colgan to cover in order to score. He wasn't sure the depleted Trojan defense could hold them.

On the first play of the series, the Panthers ran the ball for 10 yards and a first down. Second play, the QB tucked the ball under his arm and ran. The quarterback keeper play was good for another 10 yards and another first down. Third play, another quarterback keep, but this time the defense picked it up and smothered the run at the line of scrimmage. A short run play followed by an incomplete pass into the end zone meant the Panthers were facing third down.

The Girard coaches willed their defense to dig in and make their opponents settle for a field goal. The Panther quarterback dropped back and threw a perfect pass to his receiver for another first down, putting them within yards of the goal line. Colgan quickly lined up as the game clock counted down to halftime. A pass to the far corner of the end zone was caught for six points. The PAT added another, and the Panthers increased their lead to 21-13 as the final seconds of the half ticked away.

The Trojans went into the locker room exhausted and discouraged.

"We're giving this game away," Coach Bauer began, frustrated.

"High snap on a punt gives them the ball on our 30-yard line. Seven points. A fumble on our 40 gives them another seven. Missed tackles on a kickoff return, yet another seven points. They've never had to drive more than half the field! Our miscues and mistakes are giving them opportunities, and you can't do that with a good football team! We've got to settle down and play."

The second half began with a deep kickoff to Darian Kelly, who returned the ball almost to midfield. The long run was a morale booster and also gave the Trojans the field position they had lacked so far. Short runs on first and second downs left the Trojans facing third and long. Dependent on the pass to pick up a first down, Tyler dropped back and aired it out. Intercepted. Coach Bauer pinched up his face and motioned to the defense to get on the field.

Neither team had much luck moving the ball in the second half, and neither team saw the end zone for the rest of the game. Both managed to tack three points onto their scores with successful field goals for a final score of 24-16, Colgan.

The loss was a gut punch for the Trojans. They were sure that this was their year to finally defeat the Panthers. Although they had not verbalized it, many felt that under the extraordinary circumstances, it was their destiny. They wanted so badly to honor their beloved Coach with a victory over the one team who, year in and year out, seemed to have Girard's number. Their emotions raged within them.

For many of the Trojans, animosity toward their opponents

sat just below the surface as the two teams headed toward one another to swap traditional "good game" sentiments. As the players took off their helmets and neared one another, the angry Trojans sensed the compassion and heartache the Colgan players and fans were experiencing because of Coach Crespino's loss. The caustic bitterness melted away, and they exchanged genuine and heartfelt condolences as they mingled and visited with the opposition. The intimate assembly reminded them that some things were bigger than the game. More than most, Craig Crespino understood that football could make family out of strangers, and they were sure he was smiling down on them at that moment.

CHAPTER 21

Driven to Be the Best

"As I've grown up, I've come to realize that 'success' is not measured by money or possessions, but rather by the positive impact you have on those around you. For that reason, Coach was one of the most successful men I've known. I pray my sons are as lucky as I was to have a man outside of our home and family be so important to them."

- Seth Newton, GHS Class of 2004

As endearing as the post-game gathering with Colgan was, the air on the bus ride back to Girard afterward was thick with disappointment. There was little conversation among the players. They had not played their best and they knew it. They had let themselves down, and they felt they had let Coach down. Coach Crespino *and* Coach Bauer.

The loss to Colgan was an eye-opener for the Trojan

players. They had the will to win and the talent to win, but they still lacked something fundamental and realized they had much work to do. The team as a whole became even more driven to be the best they could be, and they were ready to do whatever was necessary to reach their potential.

The loss had another positive aspect as well. The pressure on the Trojans to achieve the perfect, undefeated season was now gone. The players had been keenly aware of the unspoken question that existed in the minds of all: *Will the Trojans pull off the perfect season in honor of their fallen coach?* No one wanted to add to the tremendous pressure on the boys, but the expectation loomed large. After the Colgan game, that elephant had left the room.

Coach Bauer understood the toll the loss had taken on the players, but he was pleased to see them respond with steadfast fortitude. The Colgan game had changed his mentality in regard to expectations. This group of young men possessed an extraordinary amount of talent, and he refused to let them come up short of their potential again. He recognized that the critical component the team was missing was the mental game, and he was determined to address this before their upcoming matchup against the Erie Red Devils.

Monday's practice was serious and grueling. The Trojan coaches stressed the importance of finishing your assignment, resisting fatigue, giving 100 percent until the game clock reads 00:00. They talked about the advantage of the short field and what it takes to be the team that possesses that advantage.

Coach Bauer also talked about what they had done right during the Colgan game. While watching game film that week, he pointed out all of the good things that were happening across the field and assured them that every single player was getting better every week.

"Football is sometimes a game of just a few plays," he told the team. "If we make a couple more good plays, it can turn the outcome of the game in our favor. The more consistently every one of you does the right thing, the more games we win. It's that simple."

The players had come to trust their new coach completely. He had become their rock, and they devoured his every word. His commitment and encouragement allowed them to grow as individuals and as a team.

The Trojans were gaining confidence and refused to let one loss prevent them from exceeding all expectations for the season. It was their way of channeling their grief and using it as fuel for the fire within them. Honoring their beloved Coach and the hopes he had for them consumed them. They would not succumb to hardship or pain or even failure.

In reality, it was what they had to do to keep from breaking. It kept them focused and gave them a purpose. Whether they understood it at the time or not, it was their salvation. The brotherhood of the team became a lifeboat in which they all were being rescued.

The arduous practices continued all week, and by Friday night the Girard Trojans were eager to take on their next opponent. The Erie Red Devils proved no match for the hungry Trojans. Amassing a whopping 534 yards of offense over the course of the competition, the Trojans looked sharp and fundamentally sound. The impressive 57-14 victory over the Red Devils brought the Trojans' record to 4-1.

The following week the Trojans traveled to Baxter Springs, Kansas, to take on the Lions. It was not their best game of the season, accruing multiple penalties, including one for unsportsmanlike conduct. Emotions were running high—on both sides of the field. Coach Bauer looked to his quarterback to be a leader and keep the team focused.

"I'm counting on you to step up and draw some lines," Coach Bauer told Tyler. "This is your team, and they're going to follow your lead. Take care of business."

Tyler took the charge to heart. With a reputation for being a bit of a hothead himself, his duty to rein in his teammates' emotional outbursts was not necessarily a comfortable one for the competitive young man. But he had come to respect Coach Bauer tremendously and trusted him to know and do what was best for the team.

The Trojans pulled it together and with just minutes left on the game clock held a 33-25 lead. But the Lions refused to quit. They fought their way down the field to the Trojan 5-yard line, threatening to score with mere seconds left in the game. A touchdown and two-point conversion would tie the score and send the game into overtime. Facing fourth and goal, Baxter's quarterback took the snap for one final attempt at the end zone. Before he could execute, Trojan defensive end Mike Cook ripped through the Lion offensive line and dropped him for a sack. The visitors' stands erupted as Girard took over on downs. The Trojans were now 5-1.

Their next matchup would be against the Southeast Lancers, the first of three tough district games which fell at the end of the regular season schedule. The Trojans knew they would have to knock off Southeast if they hoped to make the playoffs.

Lancer head coach Bryan Burdette had been Galena's defensive coordinator while Coach Bauer was their head football coach. Bryan was invaluable to the Bauers as they settled in their new community and Blaise took on the many responsibilities of head coach and assistant principal. In the years since Blaise had left Galena, Bryan had become an accomplished head coach and Blaise knew the Trojans would have to come prepared and play well to defeat the Lancers.

Southeast ran a Wing-T offense, which the Trojans had not faced before. Defensively, practice and preparations that week focused on identifying tendencies of the unfamiliar formation. Offensively, the team focused on eliminating penalties and controlling the ball. The Trojan coaches felt confident that the team that maintained possession of the ball, controlled the clock, and kept the other team's offense off the field would win the contest. They turned out to be right.

The Lancers were able to control the ball offensively for the majority of the first half. Rushing for 143 yards, they kept the ball on the ground and ate up the clock. By halftime they had a 13-7 lead. The undeterred Trojans came out strong in the second half, shutting down the Lancer offense and putting 14 unanswered points on the board. With the 21-13 victory over Southeast, the Trojans advanced to 6-1.

The following Friday, Girard faced the Pittsburg Purple Dragons in their second district game of the season. Typically in 5A classification for Kansas school size, Pittsburg High School's enrollment dipped just low enough to put them in the state's 4A division with the Trojans this year. Although Pittsburg almost tripled Girard's enrollment numbers, the Dragons were nonetheless district opponents, giving the game playoff implications. The Dragons had defeated the Columbus Titans the week prior so were also 1-0 in district play coming into the evening's contest. The winner of this matchup was assured a playoff berth while the loser would have to win their final district game in order to see postseason play.

Mild October temperatures and playoff implications were reason enough for fans to pack the stands at Hutchinson Field in Pittsburg that Friday night. Hopeful for an exciting game, spectators were stunned when the Girard Trojans gave up 21 points in the first ten minutes of the game. The determined Trojans refused to give up, however, and went on to outscore the Dragons 27-21 in the remaining three quarters. But the initial deficit could not be overcome, and the Trojans fell to Pittsburg, 42-27.

Now 6-2, with a 1-1 record in district play, Girard would have to defeat the Columbus Titans in their final game of the regular season to keep their playoff hopes alive.

Senior Mike Cook was upset with himself after the loss to Pittsburg. He went, as he had done almost every day since July 26, to Coach Crespino's grave.

"I'm sorry I'm not playing my best, Coach," the young man said gloomily. "We've got Columbus this week, and we have to beat them to get into the playoffs. I know you've got high expectations for us, and I don't want to let you down. I think I'm ready to play like myself again. I want to make you proud."

The solemn figure lingered in the darkness and recited the Lord's Prayer.

"I'll be back to tell you how the game went."

The Trojans practiced hard that week. The Titans' offense relied heavily on the pass, which could move the ball quickly without using a lot of game time. Girard's strategy would be to run the ball at their opponent in order to control the clock and avoid turnovers. They wanted to maintain possession and keep the opposing offense off the field.

"We're going to keep it on the ground and control the ball," Coach Bauer told the Trojan offense. "We're not going to the air unless we need to."

The Trojans had suffered two losses during the season—two games in which they had multiple turnovers. It was imperative that they protect the football. The 7-1 Titans were going to do their best to disrupt that plan and crush Girard's playoff hopes. It promised to be a whale of a game.

The final contest of the season always takes place on a Thursday night rather than a Friday. This gives the victor an extra day to prepare for their first playoff game, which is scheduled for the following Tuesday. The Trojans and Titans alike had one less day of practice before their impending showdown, which made for a hectic week.

The Trojan coaches worked tirelessly studying game films, analyzing their opponent, and preparing their team. They wanted a playoff berth for this group of young men possibly more than they had ever wanted it for any team. These boys had worked so hard and overcome so much. They had honored Coach Crespino in the only way they knew how, by giving 100 percent to this season and this team. His team. They wanted nothing more than to continue playing, and their coaches were going to do everything in their power to make that happen.

The Columbus Titans arrived at Frank Jameson Field in Girard fired up and ready to play. They were primarily a passing offense, so when they came out running the ball in the first half, the Trojans were caught off guard. The Titans put together an impressive first drive. In nine plays they marched 71 yards down the field for a touchdown—without throwing a single pass.

The Trojan offense, on the other hand, floundered a bit initially, moving the ball consistently but not putting up any points in the first quarter. Finally, in the second quarter Tyler Bennett, who also played defensive back for the Trojans, intercepted a Titan pass to set up the team's first scoring drive. The ensuing Girard touchdown tied the game at 7-7.

The tough Trojan defense stifled the Titans' next possession, and soon the offense was back on the field. On the third play of the series, Darian broke loose for a 56-yard rushing touchdown, giving Girard a 14-7 lead.

By the second half the Trojans were in control, and the Titans had resorted back to passing the ball in a desperate attempt to stay in the game. In the end the Trojans prevailed 32-21 and clinched their first playoff berth since 2003.

The team was ecstatic! The stands emptied as euphoric fans poured out onto the field to celebrate with the players and coaches. It was joyful pandemonium. A desperately difficult season had culminated in befitting success and a chance to continue fighting to make Coach Crespino proud. The entirety of southeast Kansas was inspired by the team's tenacity and their love for their fallen Coach.

Throughout the football season there was a growing sense that something special was happening, as if Craig were somehow present, influencing circumstances. The team had felt his presence from the first day of camp when they spotted the white bird. Wearing the new uniforms he had chosen for them felt like carrying him onto the field with them every Friday night. A few players had experienced strange phenomena since Craig's death, all agreeing the incidents had brought them a sense of peace. They were sure it was Coach letting them know he was okay—and they would be, too.

Some speculated it was divine intervention seeing the community through their collective sorrow. Or maybe it was simply the result of energies aligning to accomplish a common goal. Perhaps it was destiny. Fate. Circumstance.

Whatever it was, it was magical.

The team felt it.

The coaches felt it.

The town felt it.

And the Crespino family was uplifted by it.

CHAPTER 22

Bi-District Showdown

"On game day, Craig called every coach in southeast Kansas and southwest Missouri to wish them luck. No one enjoyed game day as much as Coach Crespino."

- Chuck Smith, Craig's friend and former St. Mary's Colgan head football coach

Immediately following the Columbus victory, Coach Bauer and trainers Jace Cobb and Brian Holt loaded into the school van to meet and trade game films with the head coach of the Labette County Grizzlies. Playoff brackets were in place prior to the final regular season games, so Thursday's winners knew immediately who their first playoff opponents would be. Typically, game films were exchanged among coaches the morning after a game, but once the playoffs began and the schedule became condensed, there was no time to waste.

Coaches made plans to meet after each game to give themselves more time to study their upcoming opponents.

Once again, as his family slept, Blaise spent time watching film and preparing for the Trojans' first playoff game in three years. In many ways he was surprised to find himself preparing for the postseason. At the beginning of the season, the interim coach was simply taking one game at a time and hoping for the best. He recognized that the 2006 Trojans had some talent, but under the circumstances, he felt the season would be a success if they could just get through it without falling apart. He was incredibly proud of this group of young men and the character they had displayed by rising to the challenge and overcoming adversity in honor of their beloved Coach.

The playoffs would present a daunting new set of hurdles for the Trojans, however. The Kansas State High School Activities Association classified schools from 1A to 6A, depending on enrollment numbers. In the broad statewide 4A classification, Girard was the one of the smallest schools and would be facing schools with up to three times more students. Their first opponent, Labette County High School, had more than twice as many students as Girard High School.

In addition to greater numbers, the Labette County Grizzlies had gained a dynamic new transfer halfway through the season, and the strong, bulky running back was averaging more than 200 yards per game. The Grizzlies had lost only one game since the arrival of their new impact player and were undefeated in their district.

Thursday's Class 4A bi-district playoff game would be hosted by Labette County High School in Altamont, Kansas. Home-field advantage was always an asset and a confidence booster. The Trojans would have liked to have started post-season play on their own turf, but they took the minor setback in stride. They had overcome a tremendous number of obstacles this football season, and playing on the road would not intimidate them. A shortened week of practice meant less time to prepare for this first playoff game as well as increased intensity at practice. Again, the Trojans were unfazed. They were on a mission and were prepared to do whatever was necessary to see it through.

Thursday, October 31, was a formidable Halloween night in southeast Kansas. Wind gusts at Lucas Field in Altamont topped 15 miles an hour and made the already chilly temperatures feel downright bitter. The Trojan faithful bundled up and made the 30-mile drive to the home of the Labette County Grizzlies. Their gloved hands beat out a muffled ovation as the Trojans took the field. The cold, fall wind whipped through the stadium, but the Girard Trojans were warmed up and ready to play as the game clock was set for kickoff.

The Trojans took their first possession of the game 65 yards down the field and into the end zone to take an early 7-0 lead. The drive was capped off with a 31-yard touchdown run by Tyler Bennett. Two minutes later Tyler picked up his second score of the game with a 19-yard touchdown run. The Girard Trojans were on fire, now leading 13-0.

The Grizzlies countered with their first score of the night when their powerful running back dove into the end zone from a yard out after a solid drive. A two-point conversion cut Girard's lead to 13-8, but Labette County would not see the end zone again that fateful Halloween night. The impenetrable Trojan defense smothered their every attempt to move the ball.

Girard went on to score 33 points, including a 95-yard touchdown run by Tyler, bringing his total number of rushing touchdowns for the evening to three. The Trojan offense amassed 396 yards while their defense held the Grizzlies—who normally averaged just under 300 yards of offense—to a mere 160 yards.

The 33-8 win was a good one for the Trojans, and Coach Bauer was now certain the team had undergone a noticeable transformation. For the bulk of the season, they were nervous and unsure. They played rattled and had trouble staying focused. He could see they lacked confidence, and knew this edginess was because of their self-induced pressure to win. They wanted to play their absolute best for Coach Crespino and were scared to death to disappoint him.

Things were different now. The Trojan players now knew what it took and realized they *had* what it took. They believed, as Coach Crespino had believed, that this was a special group that could do great things. But it was more than that, too. The players could feel Coach Crespino with them, maybe even working on their behalf. There was something almost supernatural happening. They *knew* they were going to win. There was no reason to be nervous. For them the outcome had already been determined.

CHAPTER 23

A Tale of Two Halves

"Craig got the best out of everyone because he looked for the best in everyone."
- Jeremiah Hudson, GHS football coach, 2004-present

After the victory over Labette County, Coach Bauer, Jace, and Brian once again piled into the school van and headed out to meet the coach of their next opponent. The three thoroughly enjoyed this time together. They had long conversations and often a good laugh. They would invariably stop for fast food and make an event of it. It was therapeutic. A chance to set aside the intensity of the season and decompress for an hour or two.

Saturday's opponents would be the Louisburg Wildcats. The Girard Trojans were scheduled to host the 4A regional playoff game. The Kansas playoff system gave hosting rights for the first-round bi-district game to the team with the better district record. For this reason, undefeated Labette County was given home-field advantage over the Trojans, who had lost one district game. For the second-round regional contest, however, the westmost team would host the eastmost team. The Louisburg Wildcats resided close to 80 miles north of Girard but were a mere eight miles east. This slight longitudinal difference gave the Girard Trojans home-field advantage.

Louisburg would come into Saturday's game with a 9-1 record. They had just shut out the tough Fort Scott Tigers, 31-0, in Tuesday's bi-district playoff game. The Wildcats boasted two running backs with over 1,000 rushing yards each and a physical defense that had held opponents to just 65 total points over the course of the 2006 season.

"To be honest, nobody is giving you much of a chance of beating this team," Coach Bauer told the team at their first practice early that week. "Without a doubt, they have the best defense we've seen this year." He then smiled at the group of young men and added, "But you *are* going to beat them."

The team was gathered in Coach Jeremiah Hudson's classroom to watch film. The players assumed it would be the Wildcats' most recent game film. What they saw on the screen instead was a 1992 playoff game between Girard and Louisburg, the last time these two teams had met. A young Coach Blaise Bauer was on the sideline with Head Coach Craig Crespino. The boys were riveted.

"They're running the same defense today that they ran in '92 when I served as the offensive coordinator during Coach Crespino's first year as a head football coach," Coach Bauer began. "They've got the same defensive coordinator and aren't really doing anything different. We beat them that year, and we can beat them this year."

Throughout the week, the coaches and players watched bits and pieces of the '92 game, learning and analyzing their upcoming opponent's defensive tendencies and strategies and then taking that to the practice field and laying out their offensive plans. Louisburg had a strong run defense. The Trojans would have to be prepared to throw the ball if necessary. Coach Bauer worked with 6'6" sophomore tight end Tanner Poppe on going up for a high pass. He knew the Wildcats did not have a defender who could contend with the tall Trojan receiver if the ball was thrown high.

Unlike their defense, Louisburg's offense had changed in the fourteen years since the two teams had last met. To prepare defensively, the Trojans watched recent game films as well. By the end of the week, both the Trojan offense and defense felt confident and ready to take on the Louisburg Wildcats that Saturday night.

It was unseasonably warm for November, and as game time approached, the atmosphere at Frank Jameson Field in Girard was quite literally electric. Along with a massive crowd from Louisburg and a throng of football fans from throughout all of southeast Kansas, a cold front was also making its way into Girard that evening and severe weather was a strong possibility.

Before the teams took the field for pregame warmups, lightning was spotted, and game officials delayed the start time from 7 p.m. to 7:30 p.m. The stands were cleared, and fans were forced to seek cover. The teams sat in their respective locker rooms and waited. Players pensively watched the clock as the new start time crept closer. When word came down that the lightning had subsided and the game would indeed start at 7:30, the Girard Trojans practically burst out of the school doors.

Tyler Bennett felt himself caught up in the wild mob barreling toward the field. It was intoxicating. But when his feet hit the turf, the strangest sensation overcame him. The crowd noise seemed to fade. He looked up at the stadium lights, then at the stands, then at his teammates. He felt something happening that was so much bigger than him. Bigger than the team, or football itself. It was as if he were in a movie. A movie he had seen before and knew the ending. He tried to remind himself that there were four very tough quarters of football ahead of him that evening, and he had better not become complacent. But still, he felt sure of how the night would end. Something—or *someone*—else was in control. Forces much bigger than him were directing this movie. He simply had to play his role.

The pregame clock surrendered its final seconds and the teams took the field. After the opening kickoff, the Trojan offense trotted out from the sideline, eager to see just how well prepared they were for this formidable defense that had on average held this season's opponents to under seven points a game.

After a couple of short running attempts, the Trojans went to the air. Tyler threw a perfect 40-yard pass to Drew Cook, who took it deep into Louisburg territory. The Trojans' strong offensive line gave Tyler and crew ample time to work, and just six plays later, Mike Cook took the ball into the end zone on a 5-yard touchdown run for six points. Tyler's PAT added another, and the Trojans took a 7-0 lead.

The Wildcat offense left the benches and prepared to put on their own show. They picked up a quick first down but eventually found themselves facing third down and long. Their confident quarterback aired it out in an attempt to pick up the first down. Darian lunged toward the ball, tipping it just enough to send it vertical. He juggled it as it came back down but finally gained control and took off for another ten yards. Girard had the ball back near midfield.

The Trojans were eager to capitalize on the turnover. Coach Bauer called in the play that he and Tanner Poppe had worked on that week. With Tanner's distinct height advantage, he caught Tyler's high pass in the Louisburg end zone for a second touchdown and six more points. Another PAT brought Girard's lead to 14-0.

Louisburg took the following drive into the second quarter but eventually found themselves facing fourth and long after a headsy play by Trojan defensive lineman Dennis Souza, who sacked the quarterback for a 15-yard loss on third down. Already 14 points behind, the Wildcats attempted a desperate deep pass to pick up a first down, but senior linebacker Brad Vinardi got a hand on it and managed to trap it against his helmet for a Trojan interception. He brought the ball in and then ran another 62 yards before finally being brought down on the Wildcat 15-yard line. Five plays later another high pass to Tanner in the end zone resulted in a third Trojan touchdown. The subsequent PAT gave Girard a 21-0 lead.

The Wildcats' rock-solid defense had given up 21 points in less than 15 minutes of play after holding their previous ten opponents to a combined total of just 65 points. They were stunned and shaken.

The visitors' offense was equally flustered. Determined to put some points on the board, they furiously assembled at their own 35-yard line and resolved to take this drive all the way to the Trojan end zone. But on the very first play of the series, they fumbled the ball and the Trojans recovered. Disgusted and angry, the Wildcat offense once again headed to the sideline while Girard took possession of the ball with just 35 yards between them and a fourth touchdown.

After three plays the Trojans came up short of the end zone, however, and on fourth down, brought in their field goal unit. But fate continued to smile on the Trojans. An agitated Wildcat defensive line jumped offsides, drawing a penalty and giving Girard a first down and another chance at the end zone. The Trojans again took advantage of their opponents' mistake and punched it in for another touchdown. Tyler's kick brought Girard's lead to 28-0.

The Trojan stands were in absolute hysteria. The opponent that everyone predicted would end the Trojans' Cinderella season was proving to be no match for the magic that surrounded this Girard team!

Although still in the first half, the Wildcats were starting to panic. With just minutes left in the second quarter, they were desperate to score before they retreated to the locker room for halftime. Another futile series left them facing fourth and one, and the anxious Wildcat coaches decided to go for it. With only a single yard needed to keep their drive alive, the quarterback handed the ball to his dependable running back. The call was a good one and would have resulted in a first down nine times out of ten. However, Trojan defensive coaches Craig Siebert and Nick Cheney had prepared their defense for the move. Jacob Smith, one of the Trojans' big senior linebackers, immediately recognized the play and met the solid back mid-stride, dropping him at the point of contact. The Wildcats had come up short again, and the Trojans took over on downs at the Louisburg 40-yard line.

Within three plays Tyler found Darian in the end zone for a 20-yard touchdown pass. A successful PAT gave the Trojans an unbelievable 35-0 lead.

Just as dejected Louisburg fans thought things couldn't get any worse, the rain began. The Wildcat offense pounded out plays as the weather took its turn pommeling them. Soon the lightning returned as well, and with just 1:21 left in the half, the officials stopped the game and forced the teams off the field and into the locker rooms. Spectators were once again asked to seek shelter and return in 30 minutes.

The Girard Trojans bounded brashly toward the locker room, but Coach Bauer did not like the delay. Momentum is a crucial aspect of an emotional game, and he was not excited at the thought of losing that very critical edge. He implored the team to stay focused.

Thirty minutes later the teams returned to the field to finish the half. Louisburg came out strong, assembling an impressive drive toward the Trojan end zone, but as the final seconds of the quarter ticked away, so did their hopes of avoiding a shutout in the first half. The two teams once again headed to the locker rooms, this time for halftime.

The Trojan coaches watched their players enter the locker room, cocky and celebratory. They were stunned at how the first half had gone. None of them would ever have anticipated having a 35-0 lead at halftime, but they were not yet ready to celebrate.

"Hey! This game is not over!" Coach Bauer barked at the team. "We had all the breaks go our way in the first half, and they had everything go against them. But in case you didn't notice, there's been a momentum shift since the lightning delay. Don't let yourselves be fooled into thinking you've got this game in the bag. This is a very good—very capable—team, and they're not going to lay down for you in the second half. We've got to stay focused and give 100 percent until the very last second."

The Louisburg Wildcats returned to the field after the halftime break to find their stands had begun to empty. The disappointing score along with the temperamental weather proved too much for many of their fans. Undeterred, the Wildcats started the third quarter with a vengeance. During their second series they put together a 78-yard drive to put their first points on the board. A bad snap on the PAT left the Wildcat holder scrambling to make something of the botched play. The slippery runner somehow managed to elude Trojan defenders and find the end zone, tacking on two points and bringing the score to 35-8.

Girard's offense returned to the field with plans to keep the ball on the ground in order to eat up the clock. On the very first play, however, the Trojans fumbled the ball and the Wildcats recovered. Coach Bauer let out a frustrated sigh. He was watching the energy shift with almost every play.

Louisburg took over on the Trojan 38-yard line and the Wildcats were able to punch it in for a second touchdown.

This time the PAT snap was right on target, and the kick was good. The Trojans' lead was cut to 35-15.

The tide of momentum had definitely turned. Now experiencing their own frustrations, the Trojans struggled to move the ball. Unable to pick up a first down, they punted it away. It was a high kick and barely crossed midfield. The Wildcat offense took advantage of the fortuitous field position and drove the ball into Trojan territory. They capped off the drive with a deep pass, which was carried into the end zone for a third Louisburg touchdown. A successful PAT brought the score to 35-22 with just under ten minutes left in the game.

The remaining Louisburg fans rocked the metal visitor stands, delirious with excitement. Trojan fans, on the other hand, were racked with nervous anxiety as they watched their 35-0 lead being expeditiously dismantled. They eyed the game clock, silently begging it to move faster. Meanwhile, the Wildcats had kicked the ball to the Trojans, whose offense was heading back onto the field to attempt to regain the momentum they had in the first half.

Tyler dropped back to throw on first down and sent the ball deep. A Louisburg defender snatched it out of the air before it could reach its intended target. Coach Bauer couldn't believe it! He watched as the ball carrier ran it back to midfield where he was finally brought down by a mob of Trojans. Girard's offense stormed off the field, utterly flustered and alarmed at how differently this half was going.

The Wildcat offense went back to work after the brief stint on the sideline. On the very first play of the series, the quarterback handed the ball to his sturdy running back, who broke several tackles and eventually had nothing but open field between him and the end zone. Trojan defenders watched helplessly as the Louisburg runner took the ball in for yet another TD. A successful PAT kick brought the score to 35-29. Girard's 35-point lead had been cut to just six points.

Nervous hands folded in prayer covered the faces of Trojan fans throughout the stands. Under the terrible circumstances of this football season, the entirety of southeast Kansas wanted nothing but the best for this team. They prayed not necessarily for a win but more so that it would not end like this. They knew the players would never forgive themselves for letting a 35-point lead slip away. They had perhaps played their best half of football this evening, and no one wanted the season to end on what could possibly be called their worst.

Down on the Trojan sideline, the two-point conversion that Louisburg had managed after their first touchdown was starting to truly worry Coach Bauer. The Wildcats were now within six points of tying the game and could actually take the lead with a touchdown and successful PAT. The game clock had almost seven minutes left on it—seven long minutes to hold onto a six-point lead after they had given up 29 points in the last 17 minutes of play. Coach Bauer was concerned, to say the least.

Tyler Bennett, however, was not. He knew the outcome of this game. He didn't know how he knew, but he knew. He told himself to stay focused for the entire four quarters and things would work out the way they were supposed to. This was bigger than the team. Something special was happening here.

The final seven minutes of the game proved difficult for both teams. The pressure to perform was outweighed only by the dread of having their remarkable seasons come to an end. Tension was high, and mental errors took a toll on the Trojans and Wildcats alike. Three fumbles, several penalties, an interception—and multiple near interceptions—kept fans on both sides of the field on their feet, too anxious to sit.

With just minutes left to play, Louisburg began what they knew might be their final possession and therefore last chance to tie the game or take the lead. A short Girard punt out of bounds gave them excellent field position on the Trojan 45-yard line, and they were feeling confident. On first down the quarterback dropped back past midfield as if he were looking to throw the ball deep. Instead, he pitched it to his trusty running back, who had already scored two touchdowns for the Wildcats in the second half. Trojan fans held their breath when the gifted athlete got the ball.

Instead of darting down the field dodging Trojan defenders as expected, the sturdy Wildcat reared back and threw the ball deep downfield. A trick play. Louisburg coaches were hoping Trojan defenders would bite and head toward the salty running back, leaving their receiver wide open. But Tyler Bennett was not fooled. He saw the pass coming and headed toward the route. Positioning himself in the right place at the right time, he intercepted the pass.

Trojan fans were wild with relief and excitement! With very little time left in the game, Girard had regained control of the ball and could run out the clock. After a bizarre game of two extreme and contradictory halves, the Trojans defeated the Wildcats with a score of 35-29.

The *Girard Press* headline the following day summed it up

in one word: *Amazing*. The crazy "tale of two halves," as the paper dubbed it, was news throughout the area.

The Girard Trojans now had the attention of the entire Kansas high school football community. This talented group of young men had high hopes for the season before Coach Crespino's death, but afterward they were unequivocally on a mission to win. This season was for Coach Crespino, and the 2006 Trojans would not be denied. They had overcome so much this year, adversity was starting to feel comfortable.

Their grit and determination were impressive, but more than just sheer will to win, there was something extraordinary about this team. Things were going their way. They were beating teams they weren't supposed to beat, bigger teams from bigger schools with better records. People were taking notice, not the least of which was next week's opponent, the Eudora Cardinals.

CHAPTER 24

Riding the Magic

"We were having an out-of-town scrimmage and I didn't have a ride or a pair of cleats. Coach stopped by my house so I was able to go, and then talked with the other team's coach and they found me some cleats. He always went out of his way to help people. It was an honor to have him as a coach and friend."
- Richard Kraft, GHS Class of 2008

"I guarantee they're nervous," Coach Bauer told the players at the first practice that week. "Nobody wants to come here and play us right now."

Under normal circumstances, the undefeated Eudora Cardinals would not have been the least bit intimidated by the 9-2 Girard Trojans. But these were not normal circumstances.

The boys smiled. They knew it, too. There was something powerful working on their behalf. The white dove, the new uniforms, the brotherhood. The feeling of Craig's presence and his effect on the team and the community was something no one could put into words, but it was undeniably there. The team didn't necessarily talk about it—and didn't have to. They all sensed the supernatural force that seemed to be carrying the team. It was comforting to know that what was meant to be, would simply be. To an extent, it was out of their hands, and that eased the pressure a bit. Destiny had brought them this far, and they would accept wherever it led them.

"You just come out and play as hard as you can," Coach Bauer told them. "If you lose, you lose. But you give it everything you've got for four full quarters."

For the upcoming quarterfinals game, the eastmost team would host the westmost team. Although around 70 miles north of Girard, Eudora sat just 13 miles to the west of Girard's W 94° 50' longitudinal location. The Girard Trojans would once again have home-field advantage, another fortuitous break that felt a little like Providence.

The Trojan coaches had started preparations on Sunday afternoon and spent hours poring over game films for this week's opponent. Eudora's offense was something the Trojans had not seen this year, and they were going to make sure the team was ready for it. The players spent a great deal of time watching film that week as well. They were becoming students of the game, and Coach Bauer was exceedingly proud of that.

Seeing the players accept the hard work required to win, band together to overcome incredible adversity, and make the sacrifices necessary to succeed at this level inspired Blaise. He had come to truly love this group of young men. The feeling was mutual. The players understood how much their principal had taken on when he agreed to coach them this year—and that he had done it for them. To help them heal. To provide some semblance of normalcy for them, and to give them the opportunity to reach the potential that Coach Crespino had told them they were capable of. It was a tremendous load to carry, but he had done it anyway. For them.

Prior to this coaching arrangement, high school football players tried to avoid ending up in the principal's office. Now they stopped in regularly and lingered long. They had a friend with whom they could talk about anything. It was pure trust and genuine love. They had developed a strong bond, like brothers in arms. Brothers from different backgrounds and different walks of life—none of which mattered. They were family now, and these relationships would last long after this football season came to an end.

It made Blaise's difficult and terribly time-consuming task of being both the principal and the head football coach completely worth it. He was physically and mentally exhausted but was not about to let up until he had seen this season through. He owed it to his good friend and comrade Craig Crespino. He owed it to the school and the community who were counting on him. Most of all, he owed it to this group of young men that he had grown to love.

Girard's weather that Friday, November 10, was unseasonably warm and mild. After suffering through frigid temperatures and brutal winds during the Labette County game, then rain and lightning delays during the Louisburg game, the Trojans were grateful for a playoff game in which weather would not be a factor.

Every Trojan victory garnered increased attention for this "team of destiny," and every week brought more and more curious spectators. The stands at Frank Jameson Field were overflowing with excited football fans as the Girard and Eudora team captains met at midfield for the coin toss. The coin landed in Eudora's favor, and their captains chose to receive the opening kickoff. The small group shook hands, wished each other luck and then headed to their respective sidelines to prepare for the opening kickoff.

The special teams trotted onto the field and took their positions, waiting for the referee to wind his arm, blow his whistle, and signal for the game clock to start. Soon the Girard Trojans' twelfth game of the 2006 football season was underway.

Eudora's kick returner caught Tyler's game-opening kickoff and ran it all the way to the Cardinal 45-yard line, giving their offense good field position with which to start their first drive. The Cardinals picked up two first downs, moving the ball steadily down the field, but the drive stalled just 23 yards from the end zone. With nothing to lose but possession of the ball, they chose to go for it on fourth and ten with a deep pass into the end zone. It was caught for six points.

Eudora would attempt a two-point conversion after every touchdown. The Girard coaches had watched enough game film to know this about their current opponent. Girard's defense readied themselves to stop the charge. Trojan linebacker Dennis Souza focused on the ball. The quarterback handed it off, and Dennis drove through the offensive line and hit the ball carrier behind the line of scrimmage, dropping him on the spot. The Cardinals would have to settle for a 6-0 lead.

The Trojan sideline was charged after the impressive defensive play, but Coach Bauer was less than celebratory. Eudora had moved the ball down the field a little too easily for his liking. He feared the Trojan defense was in for a long, difficult night.

After their failed conversion attempt, Eudora kicked the ball off to the Trojans, who were eager to put their first drive together. Starting on their own 35-yard line, they began pounding away at the Cardinal defense. A 20-yard run by Tyler moved them within striking range, and just two plays later, Darian broke no fewer than five tackles to take the ball 21 yards into the end zone. The Trojans were on the board, and a successful PAT kick gave them a 7-6 lead.

The Cardinals were unable to gain a first down on their next possession and with too much field between them and the end zone were forced to punt the ball away. The Trojans quickly found themselves in the same position, but as Tyler punted the ball off, a Eudora player hit him late, and a penalty flag was thrown. Roughing the kicker. The infraction gave the Trojans the ball back and a first down on the Cardinal 27-yard line. Girard capitalized on the miscue and just two plays later Darian broke loose again, dodging defenders in a wild race to the end zone. He was tripped up just yards from the goal line but managed to lunge headfirst into the end zone for his second touchdown of the night. Tyler tacked on another point with the PAT kick, and the Trojans led 14-6.

A 20-yard kickoff return put the ball around midfield as

the Cardinals began their next series. Coach Bauer cringed. He hated giving opponents good field position. Slowly but steadily Eudora moved the ball, eventually finding the end zone. Once again, they lined up and went for two points. This time they were successful, tying the game 14-14, just midway through the second quarter.

Darian ran the ensuing kickoff back almost 50 yards, into Cardinal territory, where he was finally brought down. The Trojan offense battled for three first downs and managed to eat up five minutes of the clock during the subsequent series. Facing first and goal on the 5-yard line, Tyler handed the ball to Darian, who carried it in for his third touchdown of the night. The Trojans secured a 21-14 lead with just over a minute left before halftime.

"Let's hold 'em!" Coach Bauer charged to the defense as they donned their helmets and headed back onto the field. He savored a halftime lead for momentum's sake.

The undefeated Cardinal offense was indeed different from previous opponents, but the Girard coaches had done their homework. The Trojan defense anticipated their moves, focused on Eudora's key playmakers, and took away their core plays. Eventually, the clock ran out, and the teams headed to the locker rooms for halftime with Girard leading by seven.

The modest lead was good to have, but nobody in the Trojan locker room had forgotten about Saturday's game and the 35-point lead they had almost given away.

"All season we've been a strong second half team," Coach Bauer reminded them. "We can't have a repeat of what happened last week."

He praised the defense. They had held a high-powered

team to just 14 points, but he also reminded them about Eudora's unique PAT plan.

"We know they're going for two every time they score. Eight points right now puts them in the lead, and in the end that one extra point can be the difference in the game. We have to keep them out of the end zone."

The Girard Trojans took the field for the second half and prepared to finish the game with the same intensity with which they had started it. Although both teams boasted explosive offenses, very little offense took place in the latter half. They exchanged scoreless possessions multiple times. Twice Eudora went for it on fourth down, and twice the Trojan defense held their ground. Each defensive stand gave them more and more energy and momentum. They were riding the magic.

With just minutes left in the game, however, the Cardinals recovered a Trojan fumble near midfield. Coach Bauer bit his lip. This is what he feared, giving Eudora the ball late in the game with good field position and an opportunity to tack eight points onto their score. The Trojans were hanging onto their seven-point lead mightily, but if the Cardinals scored a touchdown and converted the PAT for two points, they would take the lead with very little time left on the game clock.

The Trojan defense sprinted onto the field, feeling confident. On first down the Cardinal quarterback dropped back for a deep handoff to his trusty running back. Trojan defensive tackle Chris Goble shot through a gap and leveled him four yards behind the line of scrimmage. On the next play the quarterback ran the ball himself, picking up seven yards.

Two plays later, he completed a perfect 15-yard pass for a first down.

The Cardinals were now just 35 yards from the Trojan end zone and possibly taking the lead. A strong defensive stand was crucial if the Trojans were to keep their playoff hopes alive.

First down and ten yards to go, the Cardinal quarterback handed off to his power running back, who was smothered after a gain of only two yards.

Second down and eight, quarterback keeper for no gain.

Third down and eight, again the ball was handed to the player the Cardinals had counted on all season to pick up hard-fought yards on the ground. He managed to gain around four yards, but not enough for a first down. Eudora was once again facing fourth down with no option but to go for it.

With the game on the line, the Cardinal quarterback dropped back and threw a shot down the middle of the field. The pass soared over the heads of linemen toward its target. Fans in both sets of stands jumped to their feet and sucked in their breath. They watched with nervous anticipation as the ball's trajectory started downward, then ended on the turf for an incomplete pass. The Trojan defense had held their ground, and a tremendous sigh of relief escaped from anxious Girard fans.

The Trojans took over on downs with two and a half minutes left in the game. Now it was the offense's turn to preserve the victory. They had to maintain possession and run out the game clock. Coach Bauer would keep the ball on the ground no matter what. They could not afford a turnover deep in their own territory.

On first down Darian took the handoff and picked up four yards. On second down Tyler kept the ball and ran it another two. With two minutes still remaining, the Trojans would have to pick up a first down in order to avoid giving the Cardinals the ball back.

Facing third down with four yards to go, Coach Bauer signaled in the play. Mike Cook's teammates recognized the call and looked at him intensely.

"You got this, man!"

"Just pick up the first!"

They had faith in their strong senior running back.

Tyler took the snap and handed the ball to Mike. The tough Trojan runner burst past defenders before they could get a hand on him. He picked up the four yards that were needed and kept going. Mike ran the ball 35 yards down the field into Cardinal territory, picking up the critical first down and securing the Trojan victory.

The sidelines erupted in riotous rejoicing! The 21-14 victory over Eudora meant the Girard Trojans were advancing to the Kansas Class 4A football semifinals for only the second time in school history. Trojan fans rocked the bleachers as they jumped up and down in celebration. Someone above was smiling down on them. It felt as if they were in a collective and heavenly embrace, caught up in an indescribable euphoria.

CHAPTER 25

State Semifinals

"He always had a smile on his face—even at 6am practice. Always encouraging, always a corny joke, always a high five! I love and miss him so much!"
- Sarah Kirk, GHS Class of 1992

By Friday, November 17, the number of Kansas Class 4A high school football teams still playing for the state title had been reduced to four. In the more than 100-year history of the school, the Girard Trojan football team had never made it past the state semifinals game. Excitement and anticipation were felt in every household in the area. This remarkable season transcended the game of football, and all of southeast Kansas was rooting for the Trojans.

Girard would once again be hosting this week's contest. Location of the semifinals game was determined by which team had hosted the fewest playoff games that season. Although

Girard had hosted their last two, this week's opponent, the Paola Panthers, had hosted all three of their 2006 playoff games. When Coach Bauer learned they would have home-field advantage once again, he quietly chuckled to himself and shook his head. Fate continued to smile on them. Or perhaps, more accurately, that Crespino magic was still working to the Trojans' advantage.

Practice went well that week. Paola was a school with two and a half times Girard's enrollment and had a tough, talented quarterback who would test the Trojan defense, but Coach Bauer had a good feeling about the upcoming game. He wondered if the Trojans might be destined to win, and if at this time next week he'd be preparing the team for the first state championship game in school history. The thought was exciting!

As Friday night approached, additional bleachers were moved from the district's baseball and softball fields to accommodate the crowd that was expected at Frank Jameson Field. Multiple sets of bleachers were put behind the end zones and along the west side of both stadium stands as well. But it was not nearly enough. By 6:15 that evening, the permanent stands and all of the portable bleachers were full. It was standing room only. People were everywhere, four and five deep along every fence and beside every set of bleachers.

The Colgan football team, whose season had just recently ended when they lost their last playoff game, almost completely filled one set of bleachers in the east end zone. Throughout the crowd, several of Girard's previous opponents could be seen in their letterman jackets, there to support the Trojans. Coach Crespino's death was the biggest news in

Kansas high school football, and the incredible season that followed the tragedy captured the hearts of all.

As game time neared, the Trojans emerged from the locker room and headed toward the field. A small rope on either side of their path kept the mob of spectators from pressing in on them as they made their way across the packed campus. When they finally reached the field, the players looked around in awe. A thick, noisy band of spectators wrapped around the field like an uncomfortable scarf, suffocating and unnerving. A tight, almost claustrophobic feeling gripped the team. Even Coach Bauer felt himself inhaling deeply, as if in need of breathing room.

Thousands of anxious football fans had packed into Girard's modest high school stadium to watch the highly anticipated game. But despite the commotion of the crowd, an overwhelming and somewhat unsettling sense of stillness hung heavy, like the thick Kansas air before a summer rain. There was a strangeness in the air.

Tyler Bennett felt it, too. He was still in a movie, more surreal than ever, but now the outcome seemed uncertain. The strange sensation made him wonder if this was the end of the movie. He was not intimidated by their opponent; that was not it. He had thought the last three opponents were solid teams and probably better than Girard. There had been no change in the week's preparation, on his part or the coaches'.

Something was just . . . different.

The teams hustled to their respective sidelines as the Girard High School band marched onto the field and lifted their instruments in unison. The enormous crowd shifted to face the flagpole and the band began to play the national anthem. A cluster of maroon and gold balloons was released by the Trojan cheerleaders as the band proudly played. The balloons drifted upward, one by one fading into the dark sky. Most were lost in the starless night.

But one solitary maroon balloon ambled lazily, as though with a purpose, toward the flagpole. Taking the crowd's attention away from the flag, it hung there suspended in time. For a moment the sound of the band seemed to disappear.

The strange spectacle was not lost on the bewildered crowd.

"Do you see that?"

"Yeah. That's weird."

"Was that planned?"

"How could it be?"

The crowd was abuzz as the band marched off the field and the stubborn balloon finally began to drift away, as if it were time for it to go. Nancy Bauer watched from her seat in the stands as the balloon disappeared ever so slowly into the blackness. It seemed to resist the exodus, like a child persisting in play long after his mother's call to leave. The curious sight made her uneasy.

Team captains made their way to midfield for the coin toss, and the two teams prepared to start the game. The crowd noise was deafening in anticipation of the opening kickoff. Coach Bauer could sense an uneasiness in the players that hadn't been there the last few games. As before the Colgan game, they were fidgety, and it concerned him. He tried to assure himself that it was to be expected, considering the circumstances—the massive crowd and the tremendously high expectations. The amount of pressure on these young men was enormous.

Tyler put the ball in motion as he kicked off to the Paola Panthers, starting one of only two Kansas Class 4A semifinal games happening in the state that evening. Paola's offense sputtered early on. Penalties and impressive defensive plays ended their first two series, and Trojan fans were feeling good.

A long punt by the Panthers took a Trojan bounce, and Girard's offense set up on their own 19-yard line, ready to make something happen. A pass to Tanner Poppe, and a handful of impressive runs by Darian and Mike, helped the Trojans work their way down the field. At the Panther 3-yard line, Tyler tucked the ball under his arm and ran it into the end zone for six points. The Trojans had drawn first blood. A successful PAT kick increased the Trojan lead to 7-0. The riotous clamor that came from Frank Jameson Field reverberated throughout the otherwise deserted town.

Paola's offense then took the field. Their gifted quarterback had not yet found his rhythm, but that was about to change. Primarily carrying the ball himself, the young QB drove the ball 65 yards down the field in seven plays for a Panther touchdown. The PAT kicker set the ball in motion, but Tyler got a hand on it and knocked it down. The Panthers would have to settle for six points. The Trojans led 7-6 with just seconds left in the first quarter.

The two teams exchanged scoreless drives until deep into the second quarter. Coach Bauer felt good about going into the locker room at halftime with a lead, no matter how small. He was breathing easier with the Trojan offense in control of the ball and less than a minute left in the half. Things were going as well as he could have hoped, considering the concerns he had before the game.

"Just maintain control, that's all we have to do," he muttered to himself. The anxious coach watched his team move the ball for several nice gains, picking up another first down.

The Trojans got into position as the chains were moved down the sideline. They were approaching midfield with plans to keep the ball on the ground and run out the clock. A short gain on first down kept the drive moving in the right direction, but on second down Paola's defense sent the house and Tyler scrambled to escape the barrage. Nearing the Trojan sideline, running at full speed, Tyler fired the ball downfield in a desperate attempt to avoid the sack. The pass was intercepted. Coach Bauer recoiled as he watched the Panther defensive back run the ball all the way from midfield to the Trojan 20-yard line, where he was finally brought down.

Paola needed only two plays to drill the ball into the end zone for a touchdown. In an effort to retrieve the missed PAT point from their first score, the Panthers went for two. Again, they came up short, but they had taken the lead and, more importantly, the momentum.

Now down 12-7, the Trojans went into the locker room at halftime feeling the pressure. They were keenly aware that mistakes, miscues, and turnovers would cost them the game and that they had to come out sharp in the second half. Overall, however, Coach Bauer was pleased with their performance.

"You take away that one turnover, and we're in good shape," he told the players. "Just settle down, stay focused on your job, and don't let up."

The Trojans emerged ready to play. Something had felt off before the game started, but now they were sure that it was just nerves. They would trust in the magic to carry them into the state championship game!

They started the second half by moving the ball steadily down the field, both in the air and on the ground. But the drive stalled around the Panther 30-yard line, and Paola took over on downs. The Panthers drove 70 yards over eleven plays, capping the drive with their third touchdown of the night. Again, they went for two points on the PAT, this time pushing the ball across the plane. The Panthers now led 20-7.

The Trojan offense took the field but struggled to regain their composure. Two short runs and a dropped snap to the quarterback soon left them facing fourth down once again. They punted the ball back to Paola. The Panthers' talented quarterback put together another effective drive, running over the Trojan defense. Keeping the ball on the ground, the Panthers marched down the field, eating up the game clock in the process. Early in the fourth quarter, Paola found the end zone again, bringing the score to 26-7.

Now down 19 points with just over six minutes left in the game, the Trojans were getting desperate. Coach Bauer resorted to a series of trick plays, confusing their opponents' defense. They managed to pick up two first downs in a row as they hurried to move the ball while preserving game time.

Passing the ball was their only hope of gaining quick yards and keeping the clock from running unchecked. From their own 42-yard line, Tyler's first pass was batted down at the line of scrimmage. A second pass was overthrown. A third went incomplete. Fourth and ten. The Trojans had no choice but to go for it in a frantic attempt to keep the drive alive. They were quickly running out of time. Without a score on this possession, they had little hope of advancing to the state championship game.

Tyler took the snap and stepped back to throw. He launched a pass toward the sideline as his receiver raced to meet it. With the Trojans' season suspended in air, time slowed to a stop. Trojan players on the sideline grabbed each other's jerseys in angst. Coaches inhaled deeply and held it. Fans clutched their neighbors as thousands of wide-eyed football fans focused on the airborne object, now carrying the hopes of the hometown crowd. There was so much riding on this one pass. It seemed inconceivable that the Trojans' incredible season would be over without this one critical connection. Surely that Crespino magic would once again intercede, and the Trojans would come out victorious.

But it was not meant to be. Tyler's pass missed its intended target and sailed out of bounds. The young quarterback hung his head in despair and headed to the sideline.

The Panthers regained possession and were able to run the game clock down to under a minute. Facing fourth down, Paola took one final shot at the end zone but came up short.

The Trojans took over on downs with only seconds left on the clock, too little time to overcome the 19-point deficit. Coach Bauer called in a futile handful of plays and watched helplessly as the final seconds of the 2006 Girard Trojan football season fluttered into history.

CHAPTER 26

The Final Breakdown

"Girard could never replace a man like Craig Crespino. This community won't really know what we had or what we lost for many years.
- the late Dan Smith, Sr. (via Dan Smith, Jr.), Girard city councilman

Trojan fans stood and applauded their team. The mob of spectators that had filled the small stadium that evening offered their ovation as well. The Girard Trojans had played hard and given everything they had for their fallen coach. They had surpassed all expectations, and everyone was tremendously proud of this group of young men who had overcome so much.

The players headed toward their opponents to tell them "good game," then assembled one last time in the east end zone for their final team breakdown. Hearts were heavy and emotions raw. Not because they had lost the game. It was a hard-fought game, and they had done all they could against a talented opponent. Not because they felt like they had let anyone down. That was a burden they no longer carried.

They cried because it was over—being together, playing the game Craig loved, leaving everything on the field in his honor. All those things kept Coach Crespino's memory alive, and they had felt his presence throughout the season. But now that it was over, it felt like he was gone. Really and truly gone. Forever. It was time to exhale and allow themselves to grieve. Sorrow poured out, like a rain cloud of grief unburdening itself of its heavy contents. It was like losing Coach Crespino all over again.

Coach Bauer was emotional as he addressed the team for the last time.

"I couldn't be prouder of you fellas—and I guarantee, Coach Crespino is proud of you, too. The way you responded to adversity and honored his memory this season has been amazing. Thirty years from now people will remember what this team did. You helped this community get back on its feet. You can be very proud of yourselves. I want you to know how proud I am to have been a small part of this season. It's been a real honor to be your coach, and I genuinely love you all."

The affection was mutual. Taking the baton from their beloved Coach Crespino, Coach Bauer had been the second father the boys had been denied. He had been so much more than a coach to them. He had supported them and cared for them, giving them everything he had to give in order to preserve their season and help them heal. For that, they truly loved him.

This group of players and coaches had become a family. They had loved and supported each other through one of the most difficult trials they would ever face, and they had emerged whole because of that brotherhood. The bonds were powerful and lasting, and the group huddled together one final time under the sliver of a waning Kansas moon that brisk mid-November night.

Eventually, the players and coaches dispersed onto the field where hundreds of family, friends and community members were making their way to meet them. Tears flowed from every eye that had witnessed the unbelievable season, from every heart that had been touched by Coach Craig Crespino.

As they did after every ballgame, Tyler Bennett's parents and grandparents met and embraced him.

"Good game. Good season, Ty."

"The sun's coming up tomorrow," his grandmother added. This was her gentle reminder after every game, win or lose. She hugged her grandson, incredibly proud of him. The young man forced a smile. It had been quite a journey. There was so much more to process after this final game, and he was grateful to have his family around him.

Frank and JoAnn Crespino looked on from their seats in the bleachers behind the east end zone. As he watched the buzz of activity on the field, Frank contemplated the events of the last four months. It had been a roller coaster of emotions. Losing their son Craig had been the worst thing that had ever happened to them, but seeing the impact Craig had on so many lives was nothing short of awe-inspiring. He and JoAnn had had the privilege of watching the Trojan players manifest their love for Craig into an entire season of absolute determination to honor the man they all considered their second father. Frank was overcome with pride for his son, and grief for his loss.

He thought, too, about the fact that this might be his last Trojan football game, the last time to sit in the stands at Frank Jameson Field and cheer on his son's beloved team. He and JoAnn attended almost all of the Trojan football games while Craig was coaching, and they had not missed a single game during the 2006 season. But now it was over, and next year would feel different. It was the end of an era really.

Frank took JoAnn's hand and smiled. "You wait here, I'll be back." The former coach and esteemed member of the Kansas High School Athletics Association Hall of Fame started down the bleachers to find Blaise. When Coach Bauer spotted Frank, he smiled and reached for his hand.

"Hey, Coach," Blaise greeted him warmly.

"I just wanted to thank you for what you've done this season," Frank began. "You were the right person for the job, and Craig would be so proud of what you accomplished. You might not see much of JoAnn and me at future Girard events, but we wish you all the best. We want you to know that we will always have a special place in our hearts for Girard High School."

The two men embraced, and Blaise humbly thanked Frank for the kind words and well wishes. It meant a great deal to him. As he watched Frank walk away, Blaise felt a deep sadness for him and JoAnn. He knew they were heartbroken to see the season come to an end, but in a much more profound and lasting way.

Fans, players, coaches, reporters and mere spectators mingled on the field and marveled at the incredible season. It had been memorable in so many ways, some terrible and tragic and others inspirational and heartwarming. The end of the Trojans' exciting playoff run meant the end of the community's common distraction. Emotional residents released four months' worth of grief, despair, heartache and hope as they clung to each other for support.

As Blaise's wife Nancy made her way down to the field, she recalled the peculiar balloon that seemed to want to linger before the game began. The captivating form, so reluctant to leave even though forces much stronger than it were luring it heavenward. As if it were time for it to go.

That was the magic, she thought to herself. *It was simply time for it to go.*

Nancy started across the field and spotted Glenna. The two made eye contact and headed toward each other. Glenna had surrendered her seat in the stands midway through the season. It just felt like someone else's seat to her now, and during most of the playoff games she had sat with family behind the east end zone. The two women met and hugged long and hard.

"That was quite a ride," Nancy said, her eyes full of tears.

"It sure was." Glenna's face was already tear-stained.

"You know he was here with us through all of this," Nancy smiled. "He brought us so far!"

Glenna nodded.

"That's just like Craig," she began. "He brought us through all the hard stuff. It was never about winning a state championship—although Craig would have loved that!" She laughed through her tears. "It was about learning to live. Loving each other. Treasuring every day. That's his legacy."

Nancy smiled at the thought. Before long, she and Glenna were surrounded by friends and neighbors, patrons and players.

Tyler Bennett approached Glenna and gave her a gentle squeeze.

"This was all Coach, you know!" he began, his emotions raw. "He was with us. And he's okay now, I promise."

He meant it in the most literal way. He couldn't explain it, but their fallen coach had been a genuine part of this season. Tyler had felt his presence in so many ways. Positive ways, calming ways. He knew that Coach was at peace now.

Glenna smiled and nodded knowingly.

"He would have been so proud of you, Tyler," she assured him. She knew the young man had carried a heavy load during this most unusual season.

Glenna's nephew, Joseph Clark, was the next to find her. As the two embraced, Glenna imagined Craig smiling down on them. She knew how much Craig was looking forward to having Joseph on his coaching staff and that he would have been very pleased that Joseph had been a part of this season. The thought brought her a sense of peace.

Nancy eventually set out to find her husband in the large crowd. She spotted him in the midst of a throng of players and patrons. As she waited for him to finish emotional conversations, then interviews with reporters, she thought through the turmoil and triumph the Girard community had experienced since Craig's tragic death and of the role Blaise had played in the healing process.

She recalled the long hours and tremendous burden her husband had taken on. She was exceedingly proud of him and marveled at what he had accomplished. He had steered their high school through one of the most difficult journeys Girard had ever faced, as both principal *and* head football coach. He had brought hope to their community when despair and hopelessness had dealt a heavy hand.

She thought back to the phone conversation Blaise had had with the Catholic school during the spring semester and the irony of how Divine Providence had kept him from taking that job. She imagined how different the Trojans' season might have been had Blaise not been in Girard to step in and coach. She could see God's hand in all of it. He had perfectly prepared Blaise to be used for His glory in this moment, guiding his life choices and experiences. The thought left her in awe.

"There is no way to make sense of the accident that took Craig Crespino's life, but be sure that God will bring something good from it." Fr. Bob McElwee's words from Craig's funeral came back to Nancy. She knew that for the Crespino family, life would never be the same and that they would always mourn the tragic loss of their beloved Craig. But she hoped that they found great comfort and peace in the almost supernatural love for Craig the community had expressed, especially the Girard Trojan football team. This incredible group of young men had given everything they had to honor the man they, too, had loved and lost.

Nancy thought about how much Craig would have enjoyed the fact that this game he loved so much had been a healing force for the community he also loved. More than most, Craig recognized football's ability to impact lives. The fact that his beloved game had been a lifeline for Girard residents and provided a source of joy in the midst of their unbearable sadness was something she was sure Craig was smiling about, and maybe even helped orchestrate.

Nancy couldn't be sure if Craig himself had influenced the season or if it was genuinely divine intervention. Maybe it was simply the tremendous love the team had for Coach Crespino which allowed them to reach such great heights in his honor. Regardless, she knew beyond a shadow of a doubt that they had all been part of a truly extraordinary, maybe even miraculous, series of events.

She smiled as she finally approached her husband, then hugged him fiercely.

"What an amazing season!" she told him. "I am so proud of you."

"Bloom where you are planted," she reminded Blaise of the prophetic phrase that had become an unspoken mantra for the beleaguered family during that long, difficult football season. "You certainly did that."

Blaise smiled back modestly and hugged his wife. As a result of God's Providence and Craig Crespino's persistence, the Bauer family had been precisely where they were needed that year.

Epilogue

Coach Craig Crespino's legacy lives on in the small community of Girard, Kansas, and beyond. The street on which the Girard High School football stadium sits is now Coach Crespino Drive. The Girard Alumni Golf Tournament, which Craig spearheaded, was renamed the Craig Crespino Memorial Golf Tournament. Along with private donations to the project, proceeds from the golf tournament funded part of the $50,000 in renovations to the GHS weight room, now known as the Craig Crespino Weight Room.

In 2008, two years after his death, Coach Craig Crespino was inducted into the Kansas Coaching Hall of Fame after being nominated by Blaise Bauer. The induction ceremony was held in the GHS gymnasium during the Girard-Colgan basketball game, and the Craig Crespino Weight Room was officially opened for public viewing for the first time that evening.

Three Craig Crespino Scholarships in the amount of $500 each are awarded at the completion of each school year. Two are given to Girard High School students and the third to a St. Mary's Colgan student. The many donors who give to the scholarship fund hope to help keep Coach Crespino's spirit alive by recognizing students who demonstrate the potential to follow in his footsteps. As of this writing, over $20,000 in scholarships has been awarded in Craig Crespino's name. Blaise and Nancy Bauer's son Gannon, who was a freshman during the 2006 football season, was honored to be one of the 2010 Girard High School recipients. Their daughter Audrey was a GHS recipient in 2014.

In 2008, Glenna moved out of the Girard home in which she and

Craig had raised their children. Joseph and Meredith Clark purchased it, keeping it in the family for another eight years.

In 2009, Erica Crespino married Zach Harris, who she met while attending Wichita State University. Craig's father, Frank, walked her down the aisle. The couple lived in Washington, Illinois, until 2017, when Erica, Zach and their little family—Craig and Glenna's grandsons, Maddox Craig and Knox Archer—moved to Kansas City. One of Erica's hopes and dreams was to be closer to her hometown, her family, and the people she loved. In 2018, the Harrises purchased a home in Girard where they remain to this day. In 2019, they welcomed another son, Dax Joseph, to the Future Trojan Club! Erica works from home and is a practice manager and consultant for multiple dental-sleep medical clinics. She is active in the Girard community and schools.

In 2010, after floundering in college and changing his major seven times, Anthony Crespino received a text message from Tyler Bennett which changed the course of his life. Tyler shared with Anthony that he recently found himself lacking motivation to do a mundane household job. He initially considered giving a feeble effort, but then he remembered his old coach and how he would never do anything halfway. Tyler explained that Craig's work ethic and positive attitude were something he carried with him always.

This inspired Anthony. He spoke to Pittsburg State University head football coach Tim Beck that summer about helping with the football program. PSU coaches Tim Beck, John Pierce, and Brad Wells were instrumental in helping Anthony find peace. Among the PSU football family, Anthony felt his dad's presence and found his passion. "This is what I was chasing and running from at the same time," he recalls. "I was ready to be back around the game that filled my life." In 2011, Anthony was privileged to be a part of the PSU football program that became NCAA Division II National Champions.

Glenna's uncle, Coach Dennis Franchione, encouraged Anthony to get his degree and then come to Texas A&M and intern for him. Anthony was excited for the opportunity and upon graduation moved to Texas where he completed an internship and started on a career path that his dad would have reveled in. Anthony is currently the Assistant Athletic

Director at Texas Christian University (TCU) in Fort Worth, Texas, where he finds himself on the sidelines once again. He married Joanna McEvoy, whom he met while working at Northwestern University near Chicago. He proposed to her with the very ring that Craig had given to Glenna just days before his death.

Anthony still regrets the last conversation he had with his father but uses that difficult memory as a daily reminder to "appreciate what you have and who you have, and to be where your feet are, because you never know when your world is going to change."

In 2015, Glenna retired from teaching at R.V. Haderlein Elementary in order to have the flexibility to travel to see Anthony whenever possible and to babysit her grandsons. She still wears her yellow rubber wristband embossed with the word "COACH" every day.

Jace Cobb recovered from the injuries he sustained during the accident. He and Glenna remain friends.

Tyler Bennett went on to play in the prestigious Kansas Shrine Bowl after the 2006 season. Jason Spradling, the running back whose pass Tyler intercepted to end the Louisburg Wildcats' season, was on his team. The two later played football together at Pittsburg State University and were even roommates for a while.

After Craig's funeral Glenna had insisted that each of the GHS football coaches take a plant home from the service. Coach Craig Siebert's wife Tiffany, who admittedly "does not have a green thumb," struggled to keep the plant alive. However, on July 21, 2007, exactly one year to the day of Craig's death, the sickly plant bloomed. The Sieberts were amazed and at that moment knew their dear friend Craig would always be near.

Just days after the final game of the 2006 GHS football season, Blaise Bauer received a letter in his office. It read:

Dear Coach,

We would like to thank you for a wonderful season. You brought us together and took us somewhere that only one other Girard football team has been in the school's 102-year existence. We know that you and your family made many sacrifices in order to make us as successful as possible. You not only built a great team, but you built a family as well. We have become a band of brothers and you became our father.

When we were weak, God brought you to us to nurture us and bring us back together. You did just that and more. We are forever grateful, because what you did for us goes beyond the football field. You have made us better people. The fact is, we can't imagine next year without you, Coach. You are the life and centerpiece of this football team, and we wouldn't have been able to do what we did this season without you.

The Girard High School Trojan football team would love to have you back for one more season. For one more go at the gold! We know that it must be hard for you to juggle your job and football coaching with your family, and we feel selfish for asking you this. However, you have become family to us. We don't know what we'd do without our father.

The body does not perform well without the head...the Head Coach...You. Whether or not you get the opportunity to return to us next year, we must inform you that this football season will never be forgotten and neither will you. You will stay in our hearts forever. Coach Craig Crespino would be extremely proud of you and us. We are thankful that you made this possible. Maybe one more year will bring even greater possibilities. God bless!

Signed,

The Girard Trojan Football Team

Blaise struggled with the idea of serving as head coach for a second year but ultimately agreed to do it. The decision would provide stability for the school and community and would avoid additional upheaval for a team that had already experienced their fair share.

The Trojans had an exciting preseason, dazzling coaches at area football camps during the summer of 2007. But a series of devastating injuries took a toll on the team's season, and they finished 6-3. Despite the return of so many key starters and high expectations, the Trojans did not make the playoffs that year due to circumstances beyond their control. Unlike the previous year, the Crespino magic seemed to be gone.

Blaise served as principal of Girard High School until 2011, at which time he accepted the position of superintendent of Girard schools.

The members of the 2006 GHS Trojan football team will always hold a special place in his heart.

www.ingramcontent.com/pod-product-compliance
Lightning Source LLC
Chambersburg PA
CBHW050736150726
48196CB00003B/244